# HOSPITALITY!

## HOW TO
## make THE most
### of your
## MISERABLE
## UNDERPAID EXISTENCE

A NOVEL BY

# YASMINE O'SULLIVAN

ISBN **978-0-9944732-0-2**

Cover and book design by torrederoche.com

*For all the hospos*
*and Chris.*

# CAFÉ CINQUE

Café/Restaurant/Bar

**Policies and procedures, chapter 1, section 1 – Introduction**

We would like to take this opportunity to congratulate you on gaining employment at Café Cinque café/restaurant/ bar, and to officially welcome you to the Café Cinque team. This manual will assist you to reach your full potential during your time with us.

All employees are encouraged to enhance their product knowledge and customer service skills while working at Café Cinque café/restaurant/bar. The Career Development Framework (pages 16 – 52) outlines the knowledge and skills employees should acquire in order to maximise their career development potential. These can be illustrated through a combination of practical demonstration and theoretical examination (please refer to chapter 18, section 8- Pop Quiz).

At all times, employees must conduct themselves according to the Cafe Cinque Code of Conduct, outlined below:

☐   Maintain a positive attitude at all times, especially during the Wednesday lunch rush, the Saturday morning breakfast rush and the Sunday mid-morning brunch rush, or when faced with unsavoury tasks, such as cleaning the ladies' toilet after the Sunday mid-morning brunch rush.

☐   Treat fellow employees with dignity and respect.

☐    Accept that a hierarchy exists within Cafe Cinque and that all team members are required to observe the Chain of Command (see digram below).

☐   Serious breaches of the Code will not be tolerated. Refer to chapter 1, section 4 of this manual for disciplinary action taken when an employee contravenes the Code.

**Diagram 1.1 Chain of Command**

When the manager is absent, the Chain of Command is as follows:

# Quality control

As Head Barista at Cafe Cinque, it is my duty to ensure that every cup of coffee served here is of the highest possible standard. Which is why I am also the *only* barista at Cafe Cinque. To prevent the other, less talented staff from manhandling the Gaggia, I take the milk jugs and the group handles with me during my break. Regular customers know not to order coffee between 11.30 and 12.00 unless they are prepared to wait for me to finish my lunch. This also helps to ensure the quality of our clientele, as only those who truly appreciate good coffee are prepared to wait.

I am also a writer. My only published work to date is Cafe Cinque's Policies and Procedures Manual, loosely based on my favourite novel, *Crime and Punishment*.

I have made approximately 40,000 coffees during my writing career. Mostly muggaccinos.

When I arrived at the cafe this morning, after adjusting the grind and seasoning the machine, I threw out all of our mugs. As Head Barista I refuse to make another muggaccino. I intend to educate not only the staff but also the customers about coffee and the correct way to drink it. Only one person complained about the lack of mugs, so I sent her to Gloria Jeans, where she belongs.

# New Girl

I spent most of today training the new girl. She doesn't know the difference between a macchiato and yesterday's muffin so I have my work cut out for me. After a quick tour of the premises, I told her that she must keep a distance of three metres between herself and the Gaggia at all times. I then issued her with Volume 1 of the Policies and Procedures Manual and explained that as her personal mentor I will be quizzing her on Chapters 1- 12 randomly during the week. Tomorrow I intend to quiz her about the three second rule. Most employees are lazy and I use this section to test if they are lying about having read the manual. At other dining establishments, food which is dropped may be retrieved within three seconds, unless seen by the general public. But at Cafe Cinque 'the three second rule is directly proportional to the value of goods dropped' (chapter 12, section 3), which means food such as smoked salmon, semi-dried tomatoes and brie must always be retrieved.

# Longevity

A good barista needs three things to survive in this industry:
- Flexibility (body only – under no circumstances should you be flexible in your attitude towards coffee or customer service)
- Endurance
- A good chiropractor.

I rely on a series of yoga stretches to maintain flexibility, which I do at forty-minute intervals during the day. Physical and mental endurance is achieved through alcohol and prescription drugs stolen from the manager's desk drawer. To pay for a chiropractor I never ring up the first twenty transactions on Friday mornings when the manager starts late, and take the money out of the till at the end of the day. My chiropractor said I must rest whenever I feel pain in my lower back, so I rest every twenty minutes for five minutes at a time. Unless there's a rush, and then I rest for thirty. This morning I ordered an ergonomic chair from IKEA, so I can rest and make coffee at the same time.

> **Urbanspoon** I have been going to Cafe Cinque for five years now and always get an excellent cup of coffee. Unfortunately this morning's was not up to standard. I suspect the barista has not been sleeping lately, or perhaps he no longer cares for his chosen profession. I am not one to say I told you so, but it is never too late to finish that Arts degree. GourmetDi.

It's important to maintain faith in one's ability despite online slander. Fortunately, to dine at Café Cinque implies you live near Café Cinque, in one of the more desirable parts of Melbourne, so negative reviews such as this rarely affect business. We are always busy. Which is why I don't feel bad when I close early on Wednesdays and Fridays to attend Feldenkrais classes.

My ergonomic chair arrived this morning, unassembled, in a box with a forty-page instruction booklet and a set of Allen keys. The new girl has spent the last six hours trying to put it together. The cost of the chair is bound to be an issue at some point, so I have updated our Portion Control Guidelines to include San Pellegrino mineral water bottles, which are to be recycled, refilled with tap water, and resold.

## Showing initiative

While my manager is away on stress leave, I'm making a few changes to the cafe to make it more upmarket. I have implemented a dress code to discourage trophy wives from dining in their tracksuits. From now on the balcony must always be referred to as the terrazzo. All cookies are to be sold as biscotti. I have replaced outdated copies of *That's Life* with Italian *Vogue*. I have changed our weekend hours of operation, opening at 10am instead of 7. This is more civilised and therefore more European. Floor staff have been instructed to greet and farewell customers with 'Ciao', and I insisted that the new girl learn some basic Italian so she can pronounce our drinks list, instead of referring to Limonata as 'the yellow drink' and Chinotto as 'the brown one.'

**Policies and Procedures chapter 4, section 6 – Seating matrix**

Staff are advised to study the matrix below before seating customers in the appropriate areas:

Exile 1 refers to the tables on the footpath and should be reserved for mothers with prams, where their prams will only interrupt the flow of other prams.

High Priority seating (tables 1- 16) is for good-looking customers, personal crushes and celebrities. These people are encouraged to sit on the terrazzo and at the benches by the windows in order to raise the profile of the cafe. Examples of High Priority customers include Sophie Monk and Lara Bingle. Footballers and the cast of Neighbours may be seated here provided they have been involved in a major sex scandal. Staff are advised to contact relevant media publications upon the arrival of these customers. Please find contact numbers on office wall.

Low Priority seating (tables 17- 25) is reserved for ugly people and personal grudges.
Emergency seating refers to the two tables in the staff toilet. During lunch rushes these tables may be used for low priority customers, or anyone redeeming free coffee with loyalty cards. Please note that Emergency Seating will not be operational until a curtain is erected in front of the urinals.

Danger Zone includes the counter and the table closest to the kitchen door, where most accidents occur. Under no circumstances are blind, deaf or wheelchair access customers to be seated near the Danger Zone.

At any time, staff may relegate high priority and low priority customers who have displayed offensive behaviour to the Danger Zone in order to teach them a lesson. An example would be previously designated HP customer Matt Preston, who informed staff that he did not order a big breakfast after he had eaten it.

# Close Call

The owner of the cafe made a rare appearance today, and demanded to know why customers were eating scrambled eggs in the staff toilet. Rather than explain that they were low priority customers relegated to the Emergency Seating Area, I faked an asthma attack. A crowd gathered as I rolled around on the floor gasping for breath. Eventually I was given a Ventolin inhaler from Lost Property, and I did my best to make a convincing recovery, by which time the owner had left for 'an important meeting in the city.'

# Celebrity diner

The blonde girl who was eliminated in the third week of the second season of Master Chef came in today. The wait staff were very excited but I refused to seat her in High Priority. I am a celebrity myself, having been the face of *Barista's Own Performance Milk* last year. I appeared in advertisements in three issues of Crema magazine but when I tried to increase my fee was replaced by some free range cows. She ordered a skinny chai latte and I politely informed her that skim milk is for fat people and chai is for hippies, and that we don't serve fat people or hippies at Cafe Cinque, even if they are famous.

# Routine

A good barista needs a strict routine. I set my alarm for 5.15am which allows me exactly twenty minutes to get ready and five minutes to punish my flatmate who keeps me up half the night with her angry vagina music. I open and shut all of the cupboards in the kitchen, and vacuum the small patch of carpet outside her bedroom before getting dressed.

I lay my clothes out the night before; white shirt, black pants, black apron. I only own three shirts and two pairs of pants, so these must be laundered regularly. I take a few minutes to check that they are not too threadbare. I have never felt comfortable in casual attire. Even if I am in the flat all day, I will wear a shirt, I just won't tuck it in.

I carry a leather satchel from Savers on Sydney Road, which is just big enough for my Moleskine and a small tub of hair wax. Because I cycle to work, I do my hair in the staff toilet before opening. I wear a hairdresser's holster over my shirt which allows for easy access to all essential tools; a small paint brush for removing coffee grinds from the bench, a small screw driver for adjusting the screens, a thermometer, and toothpicks for producing latte art.

At work, after seasoning the machine and timing the shots, I make myself two double espressos to combat my hangover. I do this in the dark to discourage early risers from lining up outside the front door. Then I set my mood indicator, a gift from my mother: a plastic needle placed in various coloured squares alerts customers to my level of happiness on any given day. I usually place it in the last square which reads 'Go away'. I do not open the doors until exactly 7am, and if a customer dares to tap on the glass before this, I will pretend there is a problem with the machine and open a little later.

When I arrived this morning, Flat White was waiting at table 4 as usual. While I insist that staff arrive early, this is an infuriating habit in customers. He sneaks in with the bread delivery and sits in the dark until I am ready to serve him. If I am in a good mood I will let him stay but on several occasions I have triggered the alarm and told him to wait outside until the sensors have been de-activated.

As the wait staff do not start until 7.30, I have to take Flat White's coffee out to him, but he barely acknowledges me and he never says thank you. I have no idea what he does for a job, but he wears a suit. He drinks his coffee and reads the *Financial Review*. Sometimes if the newsagency next door hasn't delivered the papers yet he will pick them up. He has never asked my name. I have never commented on his choice of tie. At 7.33 he places the exact change on his table and leaves to get the tram into the city.

# The passion of the crust

A very famous actor came into the cafe today and refused to sit in High Priority where everyone could see him. Reluctantly, I seated him at a table in the far corner of the cafe usually reserved for less attractive, unknown patrons. After taking his order for a toasted ham, cheese and tomato sandwich, the new girl informed him that he was her favourite old man actor and took a photo of him with her phone. I sent her on an extended break and ran to the kitchen to supervise the making of the HCT, which he had requested on rye bread with the crusts removed. All other orders were put on hold as I worked with the kitchen staff to produce the best crustless toasted sandwich this man had ever tasted. I did my best to act casual as I took it to his table, and told him that if he moved to a table by the window he could have the sandwich for free. He refused, and I cursed these A-list Hollywood stars who shun the spotlight. Determined to recover the money I spent watching his last film, I retrieved the discarded crusts from the bin and placed the following ad on eBay:

**Genuine Hollywood Crusts.**
**Used to make sandwich for Mad Max.**
**Must be refrigerated. $15 plus postage.**

# Crush

My manager returned to work today, heavily medicated and not too concerned about the sign I have placed next to the register, 'No Skim No Soy Not Sorry.' She didn't notice that I paid myself 25 hours overtime for editing the Policies and Procedures Manual, and didn't care that rather than placing an ad on Seek.com for new wait staff, I simply called Chadwick's Model Management and asked them to send over three people with classic European features. Obviously their hourly rate is quite high but we make it back in tips. I have developed a crush on one of these models so will be omitting Chapter 13 from the Policies and Procedures Manual, titled 'Workplace Romance = Instant Dismissal'.

During this evening's staff training session, 'You say tomato; I say vine-ripened semi-dried Tuscan pomodoro', I suggested to the new girl that she draw on her skills as an actor to make our food more appetising. I explained that waitressing is similar to acting in that they both involve a fair amount of make-believe, but rather than learning an entire script, she should memorise a few key phrases popular here at Cafe Cinque – 'home made', 'gluten -ree, 'low-fat', 'no fat', '99% fat-free', 'skim milk', 'organic', 'free range' and my personal favourite, 'fresh.' I told her to go home and practice putting as many phrases as she can into one sentence, for example; 'Would you like to try one of our home made organic gluten free choc chip muffins, 99% fat free, fresh today?'

Then I showed her how to transform a menu with a few well placed adjectives.

**Cafe Cinque Cafe/Restaurant/Bar**
Gourmet Breakfast Menu
9am – 10.45am

☐ Toast – two hand-sliced pieces of organic sourdough bread served with organic butter, organic jam or vegemite

☐ Fruit – seasonal organic fruit with low-fat yoghurt (organic)

☐ Eggs – fully certified free range eggs, poached, fried or slow-boiled with organic hand-sliced sourdough bread and organic butter

☐ Big breakfast – poached free-range eggs, artisan sausages, ethically sourced baby spinach, free range bacon, home-made gluten-free basil pesto, locally sourced tomato sauce

☐ French toast – Italian-style. May contain traces of organic nuts

Please see pastry cabinet for fat-free muffins, gluten-free biscuits and sugar-free sweets.

I arrived to work a little later than usual this morning. As I walked up the steps of the terrazzo and rummaged through my satchel for the key, Flat White made a show of checking his watch. I unlocked the door and said "Sorry, some of us have lives," and hoped that he didn't guess mine involved secretly marking all the condiment bottles in my kitchen so I could catch my flatmate using them on the sly. I knew he was in a hurry but he waited patiently as I filled the water jugs, wiped the benches, polished the cutlery, dusted the register and counted the float. Then I pretended there was a problem with the Gaggia. I seasoned it six times, measured and tasted each shot and said they weren't good enough. Eventually I made his coffee, which he asked for in a takeaway cup. He left the exact change on the bench and ran to catch the tram.

Then I closed the café to tidy the office. While rearranging the filing cabinet, I discovered that Cafe Cinque doesn't make a lot of money. In fact, this establishment owes a lot of money to a lot of people; food and beverage suppliers, providers of gas and electricity, and the tax department. I will be paying myself out of the till from now on.

**Policies and Procedures chapter 3 section 4 - Conflict Resolution**

Discuss your concern with the other person involved using clear and inoffensive language. Do not raise your voice. Do not use threats or physical force. This conversation must be recorded in the Conflict Resolution Handbook and signed and dated by both parties.

Resolved conflicts: If the matter is resolved as a result of this conversation, mark 'resolved' in the bottom right hand corner of the page.

Unresolved conflicts: If the matter remains unresolved, write "escalate" in the top left hand corner of the page. Raise the concern with your superior (see diagram 1.1 – Chain of Command.) If the concern is about your superior, contact your superior's superior.

Your superior/ superior's superior will assess the situation and decide if the matter can be resolved immediately or if it requires further escalation.

Further escalation which involves intervention from outside parties may result in disciplinary action.

If your concern involves a customer, please refer to chapter 8 section 5 of this manual – Written Warnings.

When borderline personalities work together in a confined space for an extended period of time, conflict is inevitable. I prefer to avoid confrontation but occasionally I must act to correct a grave injustice. While I was rearranging the office this morning for example, I discovered that the dish pig is paid more than me. I closed the cafe while I wrote a very angry letter to management, reminding her that I am Skilled Labour. I had to do a three-day course to learn how to use the Gaggia; the dish pig just presses a button on his machine. I rushed down the road to Kinko's, where I have an account, and made several copies which will be distributed to the appropriate media outlets.

I returned to the cafe to find someone from Fair Trade spruiking ethically sourced coffee beans to the wait staff. I offered him five dollars for the Fair Trade sticker, which I have put on the front door. Next time some well-meaning hippie asks for Fair Trade, I can charge them an extra four dollars for their soy latte.

# Restraining order

I have taken out a restraining order against the dish pig. During the lunch rush I struggle to stack dirty dishes the correct way, 'Plates with plates, bowls with bowls, cutlery in the basket' (Policies and Procedures, Chapter 11, section 5) This morning he said it was not his job to stack and wash and threatened to slit my throat if I did not 'match the shapes'.

The dish pig is a classically trained actor permitted to stay here as long as he keeps his temper in check with weekly visits to a therapist. Before Cafe Cinque he was briefly employed at a call centre, but was fired for excessive use of the word 'mate', as in 'Don't hang up on me mate or I'll ram this fucking phone up your arse I know where you live mate.' When I started here, the manager told me that no matter how busy we are, I am never to ask the dish pig to help out on the floor; he can't be trusted not to harm the customers. If he wants to go outside during his break, he has to use the back door. The customers can't see him, but he makes his presence known. Each dirty plate is greeted with a series of expletives so offensive that I find myself marvelling at his creativity.

One condition of the restraining order is that he must keep a distance of twenty metres from me at all times, which makes working the floor virtually impossible, so I have decided to supervise the wait staff from behind the drinks fridge.

I came home to a very messy kitchen and a pot of "chowder"; fish fingers past their use by date and creamed corn. Amanda Palmer was blaring from the stereo, a sign that my flatmate was home. She spends most of her evenings in a dumpster outside the Brunswick IGA, where she fossicks for dinner with other like-minded revolutionaries, so we can go for days without seeing each other. I turned the music off, and she stuck her head out of her bedroom door.

"I was listening to that!"

"How have you been?" A stupid question, because I already know the answer and I don't actually care.

"Fucked! I think I have fucking cancer and my brother is probably going back to jail!"

"Oh, that's no good." She also had a monster pimple on her nose but I decided to tell her later.

"You'll have to get someone to cover my shift this week. I'm snowed under at school." By school she means the New Enterprise Incentive Scheme, which provides job seekers with small business training while they continue to receive Centrelink payments. Her business idea is a café which sells food made from 'recycled' produce.

She turned the music up and went back to her room. I noticed she was wearing one of my jumpers.

# Maimed

The dish pig stabbed me in the leg this morning, but claimed it was an accident. While waiting for the ambulance to arrive, I managed to fill out an Accident Report Sheet. Under *Cause of Injury* I wrote 'Attempted Murder.' At the hospital, a doctor assured me my wound was superficial and denied my request for morphine. When I returned to the cafe, limping and in a great deal of pain, the dish pig reminded me that he knows where I live, so I have decided not to press charges. However, knives are now prohibited at Cafe Cinque. We are only serving muffins and pre-sliced toast until further notice. All condiments are to be spread with a spoon.

Surprisingly, this is not the first time I have been stabbed. I have a nine centimetre scar on my forearm from the Home Ec Massacre of '94. Like most students, I took home economics because it was a nice two-hour break between maths and science, where I could bake scones and steal food from the dry goods cupboard. Miss Hinds considered me a problem student; someone who sought to undermine her and remind her that home economics wasn't a subject worthy of my full attention. I read Proust while she lectured us on the history of self-raising flour. As punishment, when the other students were baking scones, she made me copy out recipes from the *Womens Weekly Dinner Party Cookbook*. She tried numerous times to have me removed from the class; she said I was disruptive, had no respect for authority and no interest in culinary education. I accused her of sexism and her position was under review.

After mastering the omelette and the tuna salad, Miss Hinds

thought we should embrace modern cuisine. We were given a recipe for Fiesta Pie, which involved placing mince, tinned tomatoes and tinned corn in a pie dish and heating them up in the microwave. I left mine in the microwave for too long and when I took it out, it was black and rock hard. Miss Hinds, furious that I had not followed the recipe, instructed me to hold the dish while she attempted to remove the pie with a large knife. The knife 'slipped' off the top of the pie and sliced open my forearm. The other students watched in horror as blood squirted all over the kitchen and Miss Hinds wrapped my arm in glad wrap. In shock, I remained silent as she rushed me to the hospital in her new Corolla, insisting I hold my arm out the window so I wouldn't bleed on the upholstery. I required sixteen stitches and spent the rest of the day in the sick bay.

When questioned by the police, Miss Hinds insisted that I had tried to take my own life. Still in shock, I refused to speak, even when my mother came to pick me up and reprimanded me for ruining my school shirt.

For the rest of the year I had to spend Thursdays between 11am and 1pm in the office, putting the weekly newsletter into addressed envelopes under the watchful eye of the principal. My 'botched suicide attempt' made me very popular with the year 10 Goths, who made me copies of their Smiths CDs and invited me to midnight picnics at the local cemetery.


The dish pig has been offered a part on *Home and Away* as the dish washer in the Summer Bay diner. His mother is disappointed, as she would prefer to see her son play a doctor or a lawyer. He hasn't told her that his character is an illegal immigrant whose plans to blow up Summer Bay are foiled by the little runt from the surf club. As it is a small role, he will only be away for a short time. Grateful for the break, I have decided not to take my chances on another dish washer, and have instructed staff to throw all dirty dishes into the bin until he returns.

**Policies and procedures chapter 9, section 3 - Guide to service**

- ☐ Greet customer at door.
- ☐ Determine level of importance, seat accordingly.
- ☐ Issue menu.
- ☐ Explain recent changes to menu and last minute omissions.
- ☐ Recite specials.
- ☐ Politely explain that some menu items may take a while.
- ☐ Determine length of wait and offer appropriate reading material from behind the counter. The table below may be used as a guide:

| Toast | The Stonnington Leader |
|---|---|
| Menu items containing more than three ingredients | The Age, The Financial Review |
| Complicated lunch specials | War and Peace |

Occasionally I must remind certain customers that this is not their second home, and that they can't just sit wherever they please/order whatever they feel like without consulting me first. Before opening this morning I placed a reserved sign on table four. As Flat White went to sit down I said, "That table's reserved."

"Who is it reserved for?"

"Not you," and I placed his coffee on table eight.

Strong Soy Latte, who never tires of telling the wait staff that he is the strong soylent type, was forced to sit in Emergency Seating as I managed to rope off the entire café before he arrived. The new girl watched me closely as I poured regular milk into a jug labelled 'soy'.

"LOL."

I pointed to chapter 7 section 3 of the Policies and Procedures manual, which is stuck to the side of the Gaggia:

> Under no circumstances are employees permitted to address the
> barista during busy periods. All communication must be in writing
> and placed on the bench with the coffee dockets. Failure to do so will
> result in immediate dismissal.

She scribbled on her order pad and slid it across the counter: LOL!!!

"You know, before your time, when a person found something funny, they would just laugh out loud. Actually the only way to laugh is out loud, so they would just laugh. They didn't have to announce that this is what they were doing. They didn't have to spell it out."

She scrawled *How old are you?* across the top of the pad.

"Twenty seven," I lied.

"That's old. You're older than my mum."

"I doubt it."

"Not my real mum, my step-mum." Then she galloped off to the kitchen, waving a Chux in the air.

I tried to remember why I hired her. I took Strong Soy's latte out myself, then went into the office and retrieved her CV from the filing cabinet. Across the top I had written *NOT THE WORST*.

She is always late and spends most shifts pouting at her reflection in the glass door of the drinks fridge. She uses her mobile to take photos of random customers and send them to her best friend Tiff, with messages like "your boyfriend." She claims to be a vegan and a Buddhist but on several occasions I have caught her eating meat off people's discarded plates. She wants to be an actress. In her last year of school she performed in Chekhov's *Three Sisters*, but changed the play to *Two Sisters* "because Tiff and I were the only good actors in the class."

We have had several one-on-one staff training sessions because I am paid overtime for them, but they are pointless. She has failed the pop quiz fifteen times, and I finally gave up after the last one, designed to help her remember coffee orders;

"I'm strong, and I'm black. What am I?"

"Oprah."

I came home to a dirty kitchen and a pot of 'chilli con carne' made from Tabasco, re-fried beans and what appeared to be dog food. Amanda Palmer was on the stereo. The electricity bill I had left on the fridge last week was on the kitchen table, under twenty dollars' worth of loose change. I turned the music off and waited for my flatmate to come out of her room.

"I was listening to that!"

"How have you been?"

"What do you care? Everything's fucked!"

"The electricity bill..."

"That's all I have at the moment." She turned the music back on, went back to her room and slammed the door.

On Tuesdays, after seasoning the machine, I scan the *Epicure* for anything that may upset the manager. She does not react well to other people's success, especially if those other people worked under her when they were starting out. The *Epicure* serves as a weekly reminder that while she developed a drinking problem and earned a reputation as difficult and unreliable, her co-workers were making a name for themselves in the Melbourne food scene. One has just opened his third concept burger bar in the city, another has built a small empire peddling state-of-the-art cupcakes and someone she fired years ago for being a 'shit cunt' made the cover of last week's edition for re-inventing the sandwich ('life- altering fillings!'). While I can never hide any of this from her (she knows that if the *Epicure* is not on her desk Tuesday morning, there is a very good reason to buy it next door) I can at least prepare for the shitstorm that follows after she has read it. I am especially on the lookout for any mention of THE ONE. The one who broke her heart, the one who ran off with all her money, the one who gave her crabs. They met in a restaurant in the city; she was the maîtres-d and he was the sous chef. They moved in together almost immediately and she put all of her savings into a joint account with plans to open their own farm to table fusion gastro pub. He ran off with the hot young kitchen hand, who used the money to fund her own line of bespoke muesli. Café Cinque is one of the only places not to have it on the breakfast menu. If someone requests it when the manager is working, they are asked to leave.

Today I was lucky; an entire *Epicure* devoted to macarons. A few years ago, someone who made and distributed macarons hired a publicist. People who had never seen a macaron the week before were suddenly having latte-fuelled debates about who made the best macarons in Melbourne, and whether or not pistachio was a legitimate flavour. The manager scanned the paper and threw it in the bin.

"Macarons. What a bunch of bullshit."

I left her in the office to deal with the phone, which had been ringing constantly since I arrived.

**Policies and Procedures chapter 2, section 12 – telephone greeting**

The following greeting is to be used when answering the phone:

Good morning/Good afternoon/Good evening (depending on the time of day), Cafe Cinque cafe restaurant bar, (insert name) speaking. How may I be of service this morning/this afternoon/this evening? (depending on the time of day.)

If the caller is a supplier inquiring about an unpaid bill, use cellophane in top drawer of desk to make a crackling sound, apologise for problem with phone connection, and hang up.

Tuesday is also Yummy Mummy day. As we are situated in one of Melbourne's more affluent suburbs, most of our customers are stay-at-home mums with nothing better to do than terrorise the staff at their local cafe. Blonde, tanned, and on the wrong side of forty, they travel in packs carrying designer bags, designer dogs, and worst of all, designer babies. Cafe Cinque is not a child-friendly establishment. We do not provide high chairs. We do not allow prams inside the cafe, even when it's raining. We do not have a children's menu. A babycino costs $8.95. Still, these women insist on turning Cafe Cinque into a mini daycare centre once a week, where they can let little Anabella/Arabella/Isabella run wild and throw food on the floor while they sip their hot water with lemon and bitch about the service. The undisputed leader of this group is Skinny Latte. She truly believes that her husband will stop cheating if she drinks low fat milk. Her hair and nail appointments and busy social life leave her little time for exercise or self-improvement but if she suspects that I have not used skinny milk in her coffee she will accuse me of jeopardising her marriage and threaten legal action.

In a last ditch effort to get rid of her, I have taken to wearing a home-made paedophile's satellite tracking device, which beeps when I stand within two metres of an oversized pram.

---

**Urbanspoon** The barista should be aware that a bad attitude reflects poorly on his mother.

See below for dictionary definition of 'hospitality'. GourmetDi.

---

The dictionary defines hospitality as 'the friendly reception and treatment of guests or strangers.' But for those of us who have worked in the hospitality industry for longer than we care to admit, the word has an entirely different meaning:

- A daily reminder that no one actually cares about your aspirations to be a writer, actor, singer, dancer, poet.
- Proof that your mother was right when she said 'you need a fall back option'.
- Evidence that slavery does exist in the 21st century.

## New improved crush

The Chadwick's model/waiter with the classic European features is in a long-term relationship so I fired him. I have since developed a crush on a customer; Latte with Two Sugars. He is not my type at all and for a while I struggled to understand my attraction to him, eventually coming to the terrifying conclusion that I fancy him because he is polite. I have been working here so long that I am now fantasising about someone because they can say *please* and *thank you*. While taking his order this morning I casually mentioned that I am a writer and tomorrow I plan to casually write in my Moleskine in front of him. I also casually rewrote chapter 3, section 6 of the Policies and

Procedures manual:

A long line of customers waited patiently for their coffee as I
casually wrote in my Moleskine. Latte with Two was late but I couldn't
stop writing until he had seen me. I pretended to be working on my
novel, but I was really making a list of all the things I would change
about him if he was my boyfriend:

- Shoes
- Clothes
- General appearance

He arrived at the same time as my manager, who likes to assert her
authority in front of an audience.

"Sandy, you can scribble in your diary later. Make some coffees
please."

"It's not a diary, it's a notebook."

"Coffees. Now."

I placed my Moleskine on the counter so everyone could see that
it was not a diary. My manager confiscated it until the end of my shift.
For the rest of the day, when inspired, I was forced to write on the
back of coffee dockets.

I used a toothpick to draw a heart on Latte with Two's coffee. I
waited for him to notice before placing the lid on top, then spent the
rest of the day worrying that I had been too forward.


Today I put hearts on everyone's coffee, and made sure he noticed
this too.

When you are a service provider, it is almost impossible for people
to see you as anything else. Just as men will rarely consider marrying
their local prostitute, I'm sure my customers struggle to comprehend
that I am more than just a highly qualified barista.

When I started here, I told some of them that I am writing a book.

Now they ask me about it every single day.

"How's the book going, Sandy?"

My standard answer is "Just editing at the moment." But sometimes I pretend I can't hear them over the Café del Mar CD.

"What's it about?"

I always ignore this question because I'm not sure what it's about yet. I have managed to fill seven Moleskines with notes and observations, which I may or may not turn into a novel. The Policies and Procedures manual takes up most of my spare time. Even though I've had four hundred copies printed, it is a work in progress. I am currently making amendments to the first volume, and will attack volumes two and three later this year. Despite what my mother says, I do not have OCD. I just think that if something's worth doing, it's worth doing properly.

I have also taken to reading *The Death of Ivan Ilyich* when Latte with Two is at the counter. I leave it on top of the Gaggia and start reading just before 8am. I pretend that I am so consumed by the story that I don't notice his order at first, then carefully mark the page with a Cafe Cinque loyalty card, and place the book on the bench where he can see it, before making his coffee.

He says nothing.

As a service provider, I am also the target of highly dysfunctional behaviour. I take photos of our worst customers and upload them to the Cafe Cinque Facebook page. Skinny Latte features quite heavily. She called me a cock sucker when I refused to let her pay for her coffee with American Express. She receives a 'wage' from her husband for groceries and general housekeeping, which she spends on manicures and massage therapy. I withheld her coffee while she crawled around in the back of her SUV looking for loose change.

I call the police every time she parks in the loading zone out the front. When she realised I was responsible for her car being towed the last time, I explained that customers seated on the terrazzo and the footpath are charged extra for their view of the park, which is compromised by her Toorak Tractor.

This morning I couldn't find the reserved sign so I removed table four. Flat White arrived just as I was struggling to get it through the swing door to the kitchen. He sat at table nine, which is the next closest to the door.

The new girl arrived just after the breakfast rush.

"Sorry I'm late. I couldn't find my shoes."

I made her read Policies and procedures, chapter 3 section 4; Tardiness;

We do not tolerate tardiness at Cafe Cinque. If you are running late for work you are expected to call at least thirty minutes before the commencement of your shift with an acceptable excuse.

Acceptable excuses:

☐    Death of oneself or a member of your immediate family.

Since she started here, I have had to re write chapter 3, section 6 of the Policies and Procedures manual – Uniforms, several times. Today I included *no wrist bands announcing you were at the Big Day Out, or want to 'make poverty history'.* Café Cinque doesn't have an official uniform, because our staff turnover is so high, but I insist that employees maintain a neat and tidy appearance. This can be difficult to police. The manager, for example, came of age when the bolero was considered a fashionable addition to any outfit, and on rare occasions when Cafe Cinque hosts pre-reception drinks for wedding parties, she will wear one over her work shirt. We have had many conversations about this; she claims that the cropped jacket with oversized shoulders is slimming; I explain that she makes Cafe Cinque look like an Italian-style, European-feel cafe/restaurant/Spanish theme park.

Latte with Two arrived during the mid-morning rush, and although there were several people waiting for their coffee, I made his first.

"Latte with Two," I announced, holding his coffee in the air. A woman moved forward to take the cup.

"Not you. Wait your turn." I came out from behind the counter to put the cup in his hands. Large Mocha laughed and said "Somebody's got a crush," so I made his coffee last.

He looks like the type to appreciate Russian literature, but perhaps I am projecting. Perhaps he reads Dan Brown, in which case we could never be more than friends. In the last few days I have pretended to read different books in front of him; some classic, some obscure. No reaction.

I tell everyone the first book I read cover to cover was *Anna Karenina*, when I was ten, but it was really *Deenie* by Judy Blume. My sister had all of her books and I used to steal them to read under my bed when everyone else was asleep. The characters' lives seemed so exciting compared to my own; many of them lived in New York and went to parties and had boyfriends and they didn't wear school uniforms. After reading *Deenie* I wanted to be a model but chose to be a writer instead because no one cared what you looked like and you could work from home. I even wrote to Judy Blume for advice and she sent me information about all these great writing courses at Columbia University and Brown. I was furious when my mother said she couldn't afford to send me overseas, and then bought my sister a home gym, which she used once. I punished her by refusing to go to school, but she told me that without an education I would only ever have a dead end job in a cafe. So after repeating Year 12 at Box Hill TAFE, I studied Arts at Swinburne, where I finally read *Anna Karenina*, but not cover to cover. After almost graduating I was qualified to work in a cafe. I decided I would work during the day and write at night, and that I would be a published author before I was twenty four. That was my scary age until I turned twenty five. Now my scary age is forty eight. Last year my mother offered to help me buy my own café. "You should be earning more than minimum wage at your age." I explained that financial hardship fans the flames of creativity and that many of the great books of the 20th century were written by people earning below award.

"But Paul, those people had talent."

**Policies and Procedures chapter 8, section 5 -Music**

Music plays an important role in the running of the cafe and staff members must follow the guidelines below when using the iPod*:

- [ ] All music played before 8am should be of a soothing nature to assist staff members with recurring hangovers.

- [ ] 8am – 11am -Cafe Del Mar volumes 1 and 2.

- [ ] 11am – 2pm – Café Del Mar volumes 3-6

- [ ] 2pm and 6pm - Cafe Del Mar volumes 1 and 2.

When closing the cafe, staff may choose between Ace of Spades by Motorhead, Iron Fist by Motorhead or Motorhead's March or Die. These are to be played at full volume. If a customer complains, politely explain that the cafe is closed and that by now they are actually trespassing.

* This ipod remained in Lost Property for the required two hours after it was found on the terrazzo. The young man who left it behind has no claims upon it, despite what he says.

This morning I broke protocol and put on my lucky playlist; obscure B-sides from the Birthday Party and The Cruel Sea. I lost my virginity to this playlist in my first year at uni. I made sure the beginning of track one coincided with Latte with Two entering the cafe. This involved a long wait by the stereo in case I missed him, and a few complaints from customers in a hurry to get to work. When he finally arrived and I pressed *play,* he made no comment. So when I placed his coffee on the counter I asked, 'Do you like music?'

'Yes.'

'Do you like this music?'

'Sure.'

'It's my playlist.'

Awkward silence. Except for the music.

I spent the rest of the day going over the conversation in my head. He looks like the type to appreciate Nick Cave, but perhaps I am projecting. Perhaps he likes U2, in which case we could never be more than friends.

When I got home, there was a strange woman passed out in my bed. Amanda Palmer was on the stereo. I turned the music off and my flatmate stormed out of her room.

"I was listening to that!"

"There's a woman in my bed."

"She was tired."

"Why can't she sleep in your bed?"

"I don't have a bed." She opened her bedroom door to reveal a pile of clothes and a filing cabinet.

"Where do you sleep?"

She didn't answer and I suddenly realised she has been sleeping on my futon while I am at work.


This morning I rolled my futon mattress up and secured it with my bike lock, and went to work determined to ask Latte with Two out. I figured if he said no I could always change jobs.

I practiced what I was going to say while I seasoned the machine. I re-did my hair and checked my reflection on the side of the Gaggia. When he walked through the door I pretended not to notice but his coffee was ready by the time he reached the counter. I cleared my throat but he spoke first.

'Did you put sugar in this?'

'I did.'

'Did you stir it?'

'I did.'

'Can you give it another stir? I can't taste the sugar. It's not enough to add sugar. You have to stir the sugar.'

I no longer love Latte with Two, and we will never be friends. Tomorrow his sugar will be replaced with two teaspoons of espresso cleaner, well stirred.

**Policies and procedures chapter 3 section 6 amendment**

If a staff member develops a romantic interest in a customer, and this customer reveals himself to be unworthy of the attention, the staff member may ban the customer from the café. This can be done through a written warning, outlining the reasons for the ban, or the staff member can simply ignore the customer until he gets the hint.

**Policies and Procedures, chapter 3 section 2 – The Bell**

Over time, new employees will learn to work the floor efficiently and effectively, using the Bell as a guide. Please memorise the following:

☐   one ring – coffee waiting to be taken out.

☐   two short rings in quick succession – stop what you are doing and wait for further instruction. For example: "Dirty dishes, table four," or "ugly person about to seat themselves in high priority."

☐   two rings with extended pause between – continue what you are doing but listen for further instruction (see chapter 8, section 2 – Multi-tasking)

Remember that hot coffee comes before hot food and must be given priority. Staff must learn to differentiate between the Bell used by the barista and the bell used by the kitchen.

When I started at Cafe Cinque, I spent days rearranging my section so that everything could be reached with a simple netball pivot to save time and energy; one step to the grinder, two steps to the decaf, bags of coffee to my left, milk bottles to my right, tea bags, chocolate powder and chai in drawers below the machine. I have bruises from pushing these drawers closed with my knees. On busy mornings I look like I am doing my own private stretch class, and I will often do it in time to the music blaring from the speakers above the microwaves. Each mini routine ends with me leaning across the bench to ring the bell. The logical symmetry of this routine is ruined when floor staff ignore the bell and I am forced to keep ringing it until the manager threatens to take it away.

A few customers have complained about my excessive use of the bell, which I also rely on to move the new girl around the café. Like all young people for whom even the worst jobs are still an adventure, she has boundless energy, but lacks direction.

She is especially bad when No Choc is in the café. He is a website developer/hip-hop artist who lives around the corner with his parents. She thinks he's the best thing since low-carb beer. He parks his skateboard on the terrazzo, saunters towards the counter and shakes hands with all the floor staff like they are long-lost cousins. Today he leaned against the Gaggia.

"Yo Sandy, wassup man?" He offered his hand, but I prefer not to touch the customers. I made his coffee quickly, because he lowers the tone.

I gave him his cappuccino without chocolate, which is really a flat white with extra froth. He took a sip and yelled "Giddy up!" to no one in particular. When he noticed the new girl on the floor, he decided to have his coffee here.

"You can't sit here and just have a coffee. You'll have to order something to eat."

"I'll just have a muffin, dude." He sat himself in high priority.

"There's a fifteen dollar minimum to sit at that table, and I don't take food orders." *Two rings with extended pause between.*

"Table seven would like to order!"

The new girl pouted and played with her hair while No Choc tried to come to terms with the limited menu. When he finally found something he wanted, she took forever to write it down. She writes each order word for word; so instead of "omelette" she writes it as it appears on the menu; "organic free range omelette with sautéed mushrooms, fetta and baby spinach on two hand sliced pieces of organic sourdough bread." When a customer wants to make changes to the menu item (which isn't actually allowed) she draws an asterisk above the last word, then writes the request below, or over the page, which makes the chef a little angry. I waited for her to take the docket to the kitchen, but she lingered at the table, LOLing. *One ring.*

"Coffee's up!"

She galloped towards the coffee machine.

"Amazeballs." She uses made up words to describe my coffee,

her weekend or a customer's outfit. Well trained floor staff will find something to do while they wait for coffee; place saucers on the bench, make sure the napkins are in a neat pile to the left of the teaspoons. The new girl on the other hand, uses the counter as a barre; this morning she did a grand plie while I prepared two lattes. *One ring.*

"Table 9. Go."

After taking them out one at a time, she pranced over to the pastry cabinet and waved a Chux in front of the glass, as though it didn't need to come into contact with the cloth in order to be clean. Then she took a biscotti out of a jar and casually placed it on No Choc's table. *Two short rings in quick succession.*

"That's a black mark against your name."

"I'll pay for it later."

"With what? We're not paying you yet." She has been doing an unpaid trial for three months. I realise this is illegal but she lives at home rent-free and I figured I need the money more than she does.

"Just take it out of my tips."

"You're not eligible for tips." I opened my copy of the Policies and Procedures manual to chapter 6, section 3:

> The following formula is to be used when calculating the tips at the end of each shift:
>
> $$y(x) + Ay(x)\, y(a-x) + By(a-x) + Cy(x) - Dy(a-x) = f(x) + y(x-y) + Ay(x+y) - Bx\,(a-x) + Cy = f\,(x-y+f)$$

Tips are for front of house staff, but do not apply to the following employees; part-time, permanent part-time, or semi-permanent part-time on a contract. On rare occasions when the tips amount to more than $2.70, ten percent of this amount must be donated to legitimate carbon offset charities as part of Cafe Cinque's commitment to environmental sustainability as outlined in our Mission Statement.

There was a bit of a wait for organic free range omelettes with sautéed mushrooms, fetta and baby spinach on two hand sliced pieces of organic sourdough bread, so No Choc listened to his oversized headphones and scribbled on the back of a breakfast menu, which he handed to the new girl as she pirouetted past his table. She showed it to me, beaming.

"He's written a rap about me."

"Defacing cafe property is a criminal offense." *Two rings with extended pause between.* "Table 8 would like to order."

She headed in the wrong direction. *Two short rings in quick succession.*

"Table 8. Between 14 and 2. High priority." The numbers are attached to the tables, but they are not in any rational order. The owner's wife moves them around a lot. On her first day I explained the current layout to the new girl:

"Table 4 by the door. Then 2, 3, 5, 8, 16, 22 and 14."

"Where's table 1??"

"There's no table 1." The owner's wife had turned table one into a Buddhist shrine after a trip to Tibet.

No Choc asked for her number before he left and she spent the rest of the day in a daze. After the lunch rush, I sent her to the office for our emergency supply of napkins. Twenty minutes later, I found her spinning around in the manager's swivel chair, using the desk for leverage.

"What are you doing?"

"Thinking."

"About the napkins?"

"What napkins?" She continued to spin until I left.

On days like this I just want to go back to my flat and have a long, hot shower. Instead I came home to six women discussing gender politics in my living room. My flatmate was in the kitchen attempting to make a snack from tinned pineapple and some limp celery.

"Hi."

"I'm a lesbian."

"Congratulations."

"Don't pretend to give a fuck."

"Are the angry women in my living room also lesbians?"

'It's my living room too."

I spent the rest of the evening locked in my room, listening to these women work themselves up into a frenzy, thinking that if they came for me in the middle of the night I could use my hardcover edition of *The Brothers Karamazov* as a weapon.

When my flatmate is working at Café Cinque I avoid asking her to do anything, as all requests so far have been met with a tirade of abuse. She can only do three hours a week without losing her Centrelink payments, and she spends most of this time sitting down, polishing cutlery or folding napkins. Today I found her in the kitchen, eating poached eggs on toast.

"What are you doing?"

"I haven't had a break, Paul."

"You started work forty-five minutes ago."

"It's not even busy."

She was unemployed when she moved into my flat but her Austudy payments covered the rent. When she dropped out of Arts at Melbourne Uni, I offered to get her a job, and although she was hesitant to support "bourgeois pigs and their capitalistic endeavours", we worked out a deal where her pay would go directly into my account, so that the rent was always covered. Obviously I regret this now; her first interaction with a customer went something like this –

"Hi, how are you?"

"Fuck do you care, what do you want?"

I can't fire her while she still lives with me and I can't evict her while she still works here. I'll have to fire her and evict her on the same day. Or I could move out. This would involve breaking the lease, which would make applying for new apartments very difficult. And moving into an established share house is out of the question; it would take me months to gain control over complete strangers.

I spent the rest of the afternoon in the storeroom, counting spare copies of the Policies and Procedures manual, which helps to calm my nerves.

# Sabotage

When I returned to the coffee machine my bell was missing. I reported the theft to my manager who was busy updating her RSVP profile on the office computer. She suggested that perhaps I had misplaced it, and told me to write it up in the lost property book. I insisted it was not lost, it had been stolen. She accused me of being melodramatic.

"I can't perform my duties as head barista without the proper tools." I crossed my arms over my chest so she understood the gravity of the situation.

While she went out front and demanded that the bell be returned to its rightful place next to the Gaggia, I called Cedar Hospitality and arranged for a new one to be couriered out to me immediately. I now have a spare bell which I have hidden behind a box of sugar sticks.

# Interrogation

I made a list of suspects and when the manager left I asked them to see me in the office, one by one. I started with the new girl. I gave her the chair and stood over her.

"I know it was you."

"I only ate the top."

"Top of what?"

"Nothing."

When I got home, the entire contents of Cafe Cinque's pastry cabinet was laid out on the kitchen table; salami focaccias, vegetable quiche, lemon meringue pie. My flatmate doesn't go dumpster diving on Thursdays, she just brings food home from work. She doesn't even bother to hide the fact that she is stealing. The first time she did this I issued her with a written warning, to which she replied with a note stuck to my bedroom door: *Pot. Kettle. Black.*

Despite the four chapters devoted to theft in the Policies and Procedures manual, there is an unspoken rule between staff that we can take whatever we want within reason, although I tend to exploit this rule more than others. I like to think of it as subsidising a meagre wage. Some people get a car and a phone as part of their salary package; I have four chairs, a gas heater, a life time supply of corn flour, commercial toilet paper rolls, an industrial size tin of canola oil, liquid soap, a fax machine, two filing cabinets, rubber bands, a stapler, a magazine rack, a small freezer, bread, milk, freshly ground coffee, cake tins, Post-it notes, a bottle opener, latte glasses, and a ten-kilo bucket of sweet chilli sauce.

This morning I placed Flat White's coffee on table 4 and as usual he said nothing. As I walked back towards the machine I muttered, "You're welcome," to which he replied, "Thank you, Paul." I was so taken aback at being addressed by my real name that I hid in the office until he had gone.

The manager's office is a cavernous space opposite the microwaves. There is no door, making it impossible to hide in there and check your emails or Facebook on the ancient computer. There is a desk, a filing cabinet and a cane bookshelf. Discarded CDs, unpaid bills, letters of demand and letters of complaint are piled on top of the dusty fax machine which sits on top of the safe. There is just enough room for a chair but if you want to remain unseen by the customers and other staff members, you have to sit on top of the filing cabinet and lean against the back wall, directly opposite a grubby laminated sign pinned to the cork noticeboard which reads, "If there's time to lean, there's time to clean."

The manager threw her bag on the desk and stood in the doorway, making a quick escape impossible.

"Did you close the café three hours early yesterday?"

"Yes."

"Why?"

"Staff training."

Yesterday's training session was titled *Navigating a busy café – moving with confidence*. I set up an obstacle course in High Priority with witches' hats stolen from a nearby construction site. I told the new girl to imagine that she had to deliver a plate of food and a coffee to table 14 at the back of the room, and that each hat was a customer blocking her way. I provided a demonstration; a series of moves perfected over many years. "Twist and turn. Then slide."

She looked at me silently.

"Like a ninja."

I didn't want to overwhelm her, so I waited until she had done the course a few times before moving on to the second part of the session – *Making your presence known*.

"If you are within two metres of another staff member or a customer and they are not in a position to see you, you must yell 'Behind!' as loud as you can so that they don't make any sudden movements in your direction."

"But ninjas are supposed to be quiet."

"Failure to yell 'behind' may result in dropped food or spilt coffee, which may in turn, result in personal injury."

"This is stupid." She then proceeded to undermine my authority by packing up her things and leaving. I put the witches' hats out the back and wrote "Petulant" on her progress report.

My manager folded her arms over her chest. "I'm putting an end to this staff training bullshit."

"I can't perform my duties as Head Barista with untrained staff."

"Then train them in your own time. Dismissed."

This morning the new girl bumped into me, tripped over a chair and twisted her ankle. Which is what happens when you decide that certain procedures are "stupid" and don't yell "Behind!"

She assured me she was okay, but as Safety Officer I insisted that she spend the rest of the afternoon in the office with an ice pack while I filled out an incident report sheet.

Tables four and six cannot be moved until I write a detailed report explaining how the accident occurred and how it may be prevented in the future. I closed the cafe while I cordoned off Low Priority, took photos of the offending furniture and drew a diagram of the scene before and after the accident.

I also updated—

> **Policies and Procedures chapter 8, section 2 - Emergency procedures**
>
> All staff are required to attend a series of workshops designed to help you determine the appropriate level of response to a potential crisis. Situations covered include arson, food poisoning, faulty appliances and misplaced furniture.

We can't afford another full-time waiter, so the new girl has been using the swivel chair from the office to move between tables. Several customers have complained about the noise, but she actually works more efficiently sitting down. Before the accident, she could only carry two dirty plates at a time; now she just throws them all in her lap

and slides back to the kitchen. Drinks are a problem, as she is unable
to push herself in the chair without spilling them. Rather than run
coffees myself, all beverages will be served in take away cups until she
can walk again.

**Note to customers** If you feel the need to instruct me on how to
make your beverage, I will require proof that you know more about
coffee than I do. Please be aware that the following do not make you
a qualified barista: a certificate in coffee appreciation from the Home
Barista Institute, a half day course at the William Anglis school of
hospitality, a recent trip to Italy, and Italian husband, an Italian friend,
or the fact that you 'just know how you like your coffee'. This also
applies to those of you who drink three-quarter lattes and lean over
the counter to yell 'Stop right there!' as I approach the three-quarter
mark of your glass.

**Policies and Procedures chapter 6, section 8 – Phone calls**

If a customer attempts to place an order while speaking on their
mobile phone, they are to be ignored.

**Policies and Procedures Chapter 6 Section 2- Customer
complaints**

New employees are required to attend a series of workshops that
will assist in handling customer complaints. It is important to bear
in mind that often these complaints are unfounded, and with the
proper training, floor staff will discover that the offending customer is,
more often than not, struggling to deal with a personal issue and will
choose to focus on their 'disappointing hollandaise' rather than their
impending divorce.

While I don't condone bad manners at Cafe Cinque, sometimes it is necessary to adopt a patronising tone when addressing a complaint so that the customer knows that they are out of line. I usually respond with; "Be that as it may", "As you are well aware" or "Are you threatening me?" Over time, I have learnt to identify a complainer by the number of special requests included in their order. Requests for the following usually guarantee a complaint at a later time: gluten-free bread, low fat milk, free range eggs, grain-fed beef, high chairs, extra napkins, relish instead of sauce, aioli instead of mayonnaise, butter instead of margarine, the Financial Review, a clean glass/spoon/fork, sea salt, cracked pepper, raw sugar, half serves and mugs of hot water with lemon.

Chronic complainers can be divided into the following categories;

- Weekend Warriors – people who travel from the outer suburbs to eat brunch in a more desirable part of town on the weekend in an effort to convince themselves that the new estate in which they live really is only 'ten minutes up the highway.' They will take their time deciding between the organic muesli and the big breakfast, neither of which are available at Red Rooster, the only dining establishment within walking distance of their home. They are rarely satisfied with their table and demand to be seated in high priority areas reserved for locals. Any complaints from these people can usually be settled with "I'm so sorry about your life."

- Real estate agents posing as property developers – pick up secretaries posing as paralegals in the bar next door, and arrange to meet them for breakfast during the week. They will complain about the length of their ristretto and the type of mushrooms used in their omelette in an effort to appear cultured.

- Secretaries posing as paralegals – will complain about the fat content of their seasonal fruit platter in an effort to appear health-conscious and capable of breeding with successful property developers.

- Skinny Latte.

Skinny Latte has filed a written complaint about my attitude. It is twenty-six pages long and includes footnotes. She has provided a list of alternative careers I might like to pursue as well as the names of several good therapists. I read it during my break, corrected the spelling and grammar with a red pen and stuck it to the front door for when she comes back tomorrow.

## Written Warning

After lunch today, I was summoned to the office where my manager accused me of jeopardising the cafe with my 'dysfunctional behaviour'. She claimed that she had no choice but to issue me with a written warning, outlining all the things I have done to discourage people from dining at Cafe Cinque. She also presented me with a spread sheet claiming that my Kinko's bill exceeded the cafe's gross profit over the last two months, and that my pay will be docked accordingly. Naturally, I intend to refute the accusations and sue her for defamation. I have a meeting with Legal Aid tomorrow.

## Resignation

My lawyer has advised me that a written warning does not justify legal action, so I spent most of the afternoon dictating my letter of resignation to the new girl.

......................................................................................................................

**Cafe Cinque cafe/restaurant/bar**

To Whom It May Concern,

Certain information has come to light re written warnings, and in light of this information I feel I can no longer partake in the undertakings of Cafe Cinque Cafe/Restaurant/Bar.
I, the undersigned, do solemnly declare my resignation from the aforementioned establishment.

Regards,
Paul Whelan.

......................................................................................................................

I have made another appointment with Legal Aid to discuss copyright issues surrounding the Policies and Procedures Manual.

## Coffee cart

Finding a new job is harder than I expected. Although there are thousands of jobs on Seek, after crossing out any ad containing the words 'team player', 'all-rounder' and 'Gloria Jean's', only one remained – *Wanted: Experienced barista for full-time work in fast paced environment. Funky inner-city location. Remuneration to be discussed.*

After a brief phone interview, I arranged to do a trial, but upon arrival discovered that the funky inner city location was a coffee cart at Melbourne Central. I explained to the owner that I was not comfortable being so exposed to the general public and that I would need to discuss my remuneration before getting behind the machine. He asked me to leave and I said that I would be reporting him to Seek for false advertising, as there is nothing funky about making take-away coffee on a train station concourse.

## Food court

Undeterred by yesterday's set back, I answered the following ad this morning; *Energetic, friendly and experienced barista required for busy suburban cafe. Excellent conditions, dynamic team environment, free parking.*

I decided that my wealth of experience more than made up for the fact that I was neither energetic nor friendly and called to arrange a trial. Upon arrival I discovered that the dynamic team environment consisted of the owner and his mother, who didn't seem to mind that the 'cafe' was in a food court. I wouldn't eat in a food court, let alone work in one. I have an aversion to fluorescent lighting and communal dining. I explained this to the owner, and got the hell out of there.

## Soup Kitchen

Figuring that the homeless and destitute are grateful for whatever they can get and are therefore less demanding, I applied for a job in a soup kitchen. Although the ad stated they were looking for a catering manager, I decided to go along to the interview and present myself as a coffee aficionado, someone who can educate the less fortunate members of our society about *espresso*. I also offered my services as Sommelier during Christmas Lunch, provided they pay me time and a half. The manager informed me that they were looking for someone with more experience in a similar field, but that she would keep my resume for future reference. On my way out I noticed that they didn't even have a coffee machine, just an industrial-size tin of International Roast.

## Hole in the wall, no toilet

It is a well known fact that the best coffee in Melbourne is to be found in the many dark alleys and laneways in the city. Melbournians believe that coffee can only be enjoyed if you drink it from a second-hand teacup sitting on a milk crate between a rubbish dumpster and some stencil art. After answering yet another ad on Seek, I was invited to do a trial at a cafe with no fixed address, but was told I could find it if I turned left at the end of Hardware Lane and walked for approximately five minutes, or until I passed a huge graffitied recycling bin. Due to the lack of storage space, I was advised not to bring a bag. Although everyone was very friendly, their lack of protocol worried me. If I were to take the job, there was nowhere to put the Policies and Procedures Manual. If I wanted to go to the toilet I would have to walk down another alley and up a flight of stairs, to a bathroom shared with some graphic designers in the building next door. And because there was no room for a dish pig, I would have to wash the dishes myself. Horrified, I declined the job offer (twelve dollars cash in hand) and drowned my sorrows in a tiny bar in an alley just off Meyers Place, between a rubbish dumpster and some stencil art.

# Reinstatement

.........................................................................................

**Cafe Cinque cafe/restaurant/bar**

To Whom It May Concern,

Certain information has come to light re job prospects, or lack
thereof, and in light of this information I have decided to return
to Cafe Cinque Cafe/Restaurant/Bar.
Please disregard my previous letter of resignation, and accept
my sincere apologies for any inconvenience caused by my
recent absence.
I will resume my duties at the aforementioned establishment
early next week.
Under no circumstances is anyone else to use the Gaggia upon
my return.

Regards,
Paul Whelan.

.........................................................................................

Rather than wait for a reply, I simply went back to work as though
nothing had happened. My manager was away on stress leave again,
but the dish pig was back, having been fired from the set of *Home and
Away* for threatening the director with a large, unspecified prop. The
new girl had almost finished assembling my ergonomic chair. After
paying my Kinko's bill, the cafe couldn't afford a Position Vacant ad
on Seek, so had not replaced me. Instead, the floor staff had been
attempting to make coffee during my absence.

My Gaggia had been violated. I closed the cafe while I adjusted
the grind and made an urgent call to our coffee supplier, demanding
they send a technician out immediately to service the machine. I spent
the rest of the afternoon dictating amendments to the Policies and
Procedures Manual and adjusting my time sheet so that I will be paid
for my week away.

I decided to stay until I was up-to-date on the rent.

# Unwelcome visitor

My mother came into the cafe today and asked to be seated on the terrazzo. I told her that the terrazzo is reserved for flagship customers, so she hovered near the coffee machine getting in everyone's way. She is a tea drinker, but refuses to pay for something she can make at home, so insists on ordering a coffee that most closely resembles a cup of tea; an extra-hot, extra-milky flat white. Although I was obviously too busy to talk, she asked me if I needed any money. My manager, back from stress leave, brought her a sandwich and they had a brief discussion; about me, no doubt. My mother made a big show of trying to pay, but my manager wouldn't allow it. Usually I just charge her and ask her if she enjoyed her coffee, as I would any customer. She always complains that I make her coffee too strong but I tell her that someone with a heart condition shouldn't be drinking coffee anyway.

During my absence, the mild flirtation between the new girl and No Choc had festered into a relationship. Today he arrived in time for her lunch break. They sat and held hands in the park across the road. When her twelve minutes were up I stood on the terrazzo, and rang the bell until I got her attention. When she finally made it back to the cafe she was almost three minutes late.

"A word please."

I led her into the office. She sat in the swivel chair and spun around while I tried to find chapter 9 section 2 of the Policies and Procedures manual, titled *Consequences of fraternising with customers and other socially related misdemeanours.* Then she showed me a card he had given her, which read "I would go to zone two for you."

"So he would go to zone two, but not zone three?"

"There is no zone three. They got rid of it. Everything in zone three has been re-zoned."

"How far would he go, exactly? Would he go to Frankston?"

"Frankston's in zone two."

"But would he go there if it was still in zone three?"

"Yes."

"But the card says he would only go to zone two."

No Choc waited for her to come back out, then blew her a kiss before flipping his skateboard in the air with his foot, slamming it down on the pavement and skating off down the road, narrowly avoiding Skinny Latte in her silver SUV.

> **Policies and Procedures chapter 7, section 2 – Community activists**
>
> Please be aware that community activists operate in this area. Popular causes include but are not exclusive to: public breastfeeding, refugees, disability access, discounts for the disadvantaged, environmental sustainability, free parking, noise restrictions and equal opportunity employment. If you suspect a group of diners are community activists, cease service immediately and report to a member of the management team. If an activist initiates a discussion about social responsibility, please direct their attention to the Fair Trade sticker on the front door.

# Some like it hot

We have many elderly customers who insist that their lattes with no froth are served piping hot, so that I burn my hand placing the glasses on the saucers. Arguing with them is pointless, as most of them are deaf. I tried to remove our wheelchair ramp but our dairy supplier refused to carry crates of milk up the steps. I am now researching health risks associated with drinking coffee in old age and intend to distribute a flyer to all retirement homes within a five-kilometre radius.

# If you see something, say something

Rather than admit I was too hungover to work this morning, I left an old backpack from Lost Property under table six for an hour, then called Terrorist Hotline Australia. The cafe was closed while police did a thorough search of the premises. Although they found no evidence of terrorist activity, they did find a few questionable things in the kitchen, and suggested we remain closed for a few hours while we gave the place a good clean.

In a rare show of camaraderie, my manager suggested a drink at closing time. She keeps a bottle under her desk in the office. She offered me the only seat and perched on the fax machine, exhausted. She leaned against the wall, took the padding out of her bra, and chucked it on the desk. A former dancer, she usually sits incredibly straight but this evening she slumped against the wall, eyes closed. Her makeup was smudged. Under the harsh office lighting she looked ancient.

'Forty fucking five,' she slurred. Maybe she keeps a few bottles under her desk.

'Is it your birthday?'

'Forty fucking five.' She was lying of course. I've seen her driver's licence and she is actually forty fucking eight.

I took a swig from the bottle and realised it has been exactly five years since she interviewed me for this job. At the time I thought it would be temporary. When she listed what was expected of me, I tried to sound keen but already I was planning my resignation. Two, three months tops, then I'd leave to pursue my writing career. I remember looking at her jowls and wondering how long she'd been here, whether or not she actually liked it, whether or not she cared. I have since discovered that she remains because she can drink for free. The staff pretend not to notice the empty bottles hidden in various corners of the cafe, more out of fear than respect. She's in love with the owner. He's married, but takes advantage of her devotion, getting her to do his dirty work, so that when the tax department finally comes knocking, he can blame her.

The barista before me was fired for snorting the espresso cleaner. "Drug abuse is not tolerated at Cafe Cinque." She asked me if I took drugs. I told her no, which was true, but this is only because I can't mix recreational drugs with my prescribed ones. Over the years my manager and I have developed a healthy respect for each other, based on mutual distrust. We argue constantly but we have enough dirt on each other not to push too far. It is in both of our interests to make sure the cafe keeps running for as long as we can, because we have nowhere else to go. Most dining establishments prefer young, attractive, happy people working front of house. Neither of us has a steady relationship, we don't own homes, we have few friends. I took this job smug in the knowledge that it was beneath me, that I could leave anytime. But something changed between then and now, I have become comfortable.

"I'm just going to end it right here in this office, Paul." Birthdays have a disturbing effect on the staff at Cafe Cinque, especially those who have had more than one while employed here. They are usually celebrated with a candle in a muffin and a dreary 'hip hip hooray' just before the lunch rush. I try to imagine being forty-eight. I always assumed I'd be famous or dead by then. It used to seem so far away. What did I want by the time I was forty-eight? What did she want?

'You don't look a day over forty-three.'

'Shut up Paul. Bring me another bottle of Shiraz.'

Later that night, I had a nightmare, the same one I've been having since I started at Café Cinque; I am on the machine. It's busy. I have a long list of orders that I can't keep up with. The dockets spill out of the machine and on to the floor, covering my feet. I make the same coffee over and over again but something stops me from finishing it. Either the milk is burnt or the shot comes out too fast and I have to start again. The orders keep coming until I am drowning in a sea of dockets and I can't see the counter. I can hear people complaining about the long wait but I can't do anything about it. I woke up screaming.

"What the fuck Paul? I was hoping to sleep in this morning."

"I thought I saw someone at the window." My flatmate doesn't need to know I have nightmares.

"Oh, that's just Helga. I told her she could camp out in the courtyard for a while."

A customer died in Low Priority this week. She was quite old and she fell off her chair. I'm not sure if she died before or after her head hit the floor. I drew a chalk outline around the body and called an ambulance, then hid all evidence that she had eaten at the café.

Her son came in later and thanked us for all our help. He said that she had always enjoyed coming here, that it helped to have routine after her husband passed away. Then he asked us to attend her funeral. None of us could remember seeing this woman before. But we closed the café on Friday morning and took a taxi to the Brighton General

Cemetery, where we sat surrounded by her grieving family. Her granddaughter gave the eulogy and mentioned the old lady's favourite past time; going to her favourite café every morning for a cup of cappuccino. I was grateful that none of these people were with her on her last visit, to hear me say "No, I haven't forgotten you, I'm fucking busy. Wait your turn."

We were unusually quiet in the taxi on the way back to work. I placed a reserved sign on her table and insisted on five minutes of silence, at the end of which the manager asked me, "Do you think she left us anything in the will? Because she used to like it here so much?"

"How do we find out?"

We decided to wait a week before contacting the family.

I came home to a fridge stocked with plastic take-away containers which had been filled with tinned tomatoes.

"Gazpacho."

"How was your day?"

"Fucked."

"Do you think you could clean the kitchen, after making gazpacho?"

"No."


Today's staff training focused on the proper placement of coffees on tables. I followed the new girl as she took a cappuccino out to table 3.

"The handle of the cup must be facing east, approximately thirty centimetres from the edge of the table." The new girl struggles with east and west, even though I gave her a compass. The customer said it was fine where she put it.

"It's not about you, we have procedures which need to be followed."

"I'd like to speak to the manager."

"The manager is tired and emotional. You can put your concerns in writing, addressed to me, the Executive Barista, but due to the large volume of complaints we receive, I can't guarantee a response."

The manager cornered me in the office after lunch.

"A word please."

"I'm actually busy."

"Did you conduct staff training while there were customers in the café?"

"Yes I did."

"A gentleman complained about not being allowed to drink his coffee until you had moved it around the table for half an hour. Is this true, Paul?"

"Obviously this gentleman is prone to mild exaggeration."

"Did you or did you not move his coffee around the table?"

"I did."

"That's unacceptable, Paul. We can't afford to lose any more customers."

"I quit."

"Again?"

"I'm serious this time. There are plenty of café/restaurant/bars out there who will appreciate my worth."

"Good riddance."

"I'm not leaving today. I'm giving you the required two weeks' notice."

"Don't bother. You can leave right now."

"Who's going to make coffee this afternoon?"

"Me."

"You wouldn't dare."

"It's not rocket science, Paul. Now get out. Don't come back this time."

"I won't."

And I almost didn't. I went straight to the competition four blocks away, which had received enthusiastic reviews in *Bean Scene* and the *Epicure*.

I took a copy of my CV, which I have had to edit down to six pages now that Cafe Cinque no longer pays for my photocopying. I entered a converted warehouse filled with vintage coffee machines and beautiful people sipping espresso. The staff seemed happy to be there. No one wore a uniform, but they all dressed the same; tight fitting checked shirts, rolled up jeans, brogues, no socks. The girls wore polyester frocks, patterned tights and thick-rimmed glasses. No one yelled at the customers, no one was scared of the dish pig. It seemed ideal.

The menu included a twelve-dollar coffee, brewed from ethically sourced, single-origin beans handpicked and roasted in third world countries. A sign above the coffee machine read: *Please note that the Twelve Dollar Coffee does not take the form of a mugacinno, frappacinno or mocha chai latte.*

A waiter (facial hair and a tattoo) approached my table with a map and pointed out Veracruz, Chiapas, The Mauna Loa Volcano and Sulawesi, explained the difference between Robusta and Arabica, and described coffee using three or more adjectives usually reserved for wine. He recommended the single origin pour-over from Venezuela. "These berry flavours will hit just the right notes over ice, dude."

"I'm sorry, I have no idea what you just said. I would like a strong black coffee. No ice."

"Ristretto, straight up. I like your style."

The barista (facial hair, tattoo, man bun) placed my coffee on the table and announced its origin. I hid my CV under this month's Smith Journal and watched him as he back washed the machine before making the next round of drinks.

I realised that if I worked there, I would have to *work*. There was nowhere to hide if you wanted to make a quick phone call or work on your novel. There was nowhere to hide if you wanted to read the *Epicure* cover to cover in case you got a mention. Worse than that, I would have to work with someone who knew more about coffee than I did, and while I might learn something, I would never be Head Barista. I might not even be allowed on the coffee machine. I finished my full-bodied single-origin ristretto and left, depressed in the knowledge that the only place I fit in is Cafe Cinque cafe/restaurant/ bar.

"Look what the cat dragged in."

"I want my job back."

"You'll have to apply for it."

I bit my tongue and placed my CV on her desk.

When I got home there was a strange woman in my kitchen, cleaning the inside of the oven with a scourer sponge. A week's worth of dishes had been washed and put away, the floor had been swept and mopped, and the carpet had been vacuumed.

"You must be Paul."

"Who are you?"

"I'm Sandra's mother." She removed a rubber glove to shake my hand.

"How did you get in?"

"I have a key."

The fridge was full of Tupperware containers labelled 'soup' and 'stew'. The bathroom smelled of Pine-O-Clean.

"I'd prefer it if you didn't use a scourer. I'll lose my bond if you scratch the oven." I gave her a soft sponge from under the sink.

There was an envelope full of cash on the kitchen table, which I pocketed after she left. When my flatmate returned from dumpster diving I waited for her to say something about the fully stocked fridge and the clean bathroom. She threw the Tupperware in the bin and pulled all of our crockery out of the cupboard and smashed it against the wall.

"I'm really fucking sorry but I am really fucking angry."

"I hope you're going to replace them. It took me months to steal the entire set."

I ate my dinner out of a take-away container.

**Policies and Procedures chapter 15, section 8 – Gloves**

Individuals with pus-forming wounds on their hands must wear a single-use glove at all times.

I was a little late for work this morning, but Barbara, the owner's wife had let Flat White in. Which meant she had stopped taking her medication and I could expect to see her here every morning, rearranging the café or clearing out the office. Flat White sat at table 4 while Barbara dusted the vintage San Pellegrino prints on the back wall. Cafe Cinque has undergone countless makeovers in the last twelve months and dramatic changes generally coincide with Barbara's decision to switch 'careers'. She has never had a full time job, and refuses to work in the cafe, but offers support through interior decoration, feng-shui and visual merchandising.

Usually we just learn to work around the paper mache uterus in the middle of the cafe or discreetly move the giant Buddha which no doubt transforms the energy of the room but prevents staff from walking to and from the terrazzo.

Last month she was a fashion designer. Her first project was new uniforms for the staff; utilitarian smocks, not unlike strait jackets, which require two people's assistance to get in and out of. They were light grey, so dirt showed up on them immediately, and cut in such a way that approximately three metres of material gathered on the left side of your body and got stuck in the swing door whenever you entered the kitchen. The manager refused to wear one, as she refuses to do anything to please the owner's wife, including ending her affair with the owner. The new girl couldn't get hers over her head so wore it as a very large turban, which meant she couldn't fit between the drinks fridge and the microwaves during the lunch rush. I had to be cut out of mine at the end of the day.

Barbara's interior design phase can be divided into two categories, my favourite being "Welcome to the jungle", which involved animal print table cloths and taxidermy. During her minimalist phase she changed our letterhead paper and the sign on the door to read '5', and removed all the furniture. The owner pointed out that he couldn't make any money if there was nowhere for people to sit, so she had to put it back.

Barb also fancies herself as a bit of a socialite. Sometimes when she throws one of her infamous cocktail parties, we are paid cash to wait on the guests. This involves walking around her patio with platters of smoked trout, eavesdropping on conversations about property develop-ment and the latest cosmetic surgery procedures to come out of the US. Last time I had to cover for the manager while she had sex with the owner in one of the spare bedrooms. I find their affair incredibly stressful; although I am certain that Barbara suspects something, I don't think she knows that I know, and I know that if she knew she would be heartbroken because she is actually quite fond of me.

**Policies and Procedures, chapter 7 section 5 – What to do if a customer is injured in the cafe**

Determine cause of injury. If self-inflicted, gather witnesses from surrounding tables. If injury is the result of staff negligence, apologise and offer complimentary muffin. Do not use tea towels to stem blood flow. All incidents must be recorded. Incident Report Sheets are located in the bottom drawer of the filing cabinet, under 'P' for "Problematic issues which may lead to legal difficulties."

It was only a matter of time before No Choc ollied off the terrazzo steps and collided with Skinny Latte as she attempted a parallel park in the loading zone. He lay unconscious in the gutter as she took photos of the scratches on the side of her car, then came inside and demanded a coffee.

**Cafe Cinque cafe/ restaurant /bar**
**Incident Report Sheet**

**Incident no:** 675

**Time and place of incident:** Tuesday 8.53am, Exile 1/Loading zone

**Parties involved:** No Choc, Skinny Latte

**Ambulance called:** eventually.

**Cause of Injury:** blatant stupidity

**Number of complimentary muffins required to placate victim:**
none (cannot eat solids for at least three months)

The new girl is showing little sign of improvement so I have increased our staff training sessions from once a fortnight to twice a week. Tonight's session was based on Chapter 12 of the Policies and Procedures Manual; *Using knowledge to build customer trust, loyalty and sales.* A recent medical study has revealed that coffee consumption may decrease the risk of endometrial cancer among women of excessive body weight. I have had several pamphlets printed with this valuable information, which the new girl is to distribute amongst our larger female customers, which should result in increased coffee sales.

**Policies and Procedures chapter 4, section 6 - Written warnings**

If a customer displays unsavoury behaviour or upsets a member of staff, the management team may issue the offender with a written warning and suspend service until further notice. If the customer wishes to continue patronising the cafe, he or she must state in writing that they understand the reason for the warning and promise to behave appropriately in the future. The following behaviour may incur a written warning:

☐   Violation of the dress code

☐   Bad manners

☐   Short changing

☐   Unreasonable requests (more than two changes to a menu item constitutes an unreasonable request)

☐   Unfounded complaints

☐   Refusal to sit where one is told

☐   Refusal to pay

☐   Refusal to leave

For a full list of previous violations committed by members of staff, please read pages 189 - 265 of this manual.

This morning Skinny Latte offered to pay me to attend her next therapy session. Her psychologist doesn't believe that someone she sees for ten minutes a day could be the cause of so much anger and frustration. She suggested that I am a figment of Skinny Latte's imagination, a hideous monster she has invented who represents everything negative in her life.

After she had left the new girl asked "Do you think it's a coincidence that everyone you know is in therapy? Wouldn't it be easier if you went to therapy, to save everyone else the trouble?"

# In treatment

Skinny Latte's psychologist works out of her apartment on Toorak Rd. As she led me into her front room she said, "Call me Karen." There was only one couch. Karen watched me closely as I sat as far away from Skinny Latte as possible. We sat in silence for a few minutes. Skinny Latte inspected her nails and I studied the room; beige walls, beige desk, glass coffee table, heavy curtains. One plant. Karen sat in a chair opposite us, straightened her skirt and asked Skinny Latte if she'd like to begin.

Skinny Latte took a deep breath, placed her hands in her lap and said, "I feel that Paul goes out of his way to ignore me, and that by using full cream milk to make my coffee when I specifically ask for low fat, he is purposefully undermining me; he is telling me in his own passive-aggressive way that I am not important, that I am not worth listening to." Then she blew her nose and cried. "If your local barista won't to listen to you, who will?"

"Objection."

"Yes, Paul?" Karen crossed her legs and leaned towards me.

"I am not your *local* barista. Your local barista is three suburbs away, in a less desirable part of Melbourne. You drive to Café Cinque every day because you wish to be mistaken for a local."

Skinny Latte excused herself to use the bathroom. When she came back, Karen said, "Last week she mentioned she has tried to reach out to you in writing."

"She wrote a letter of complaint and addressed it to my manager."

"I didn't know how else to get his attention!"

"And what was the result of that?"

"I was issued with a written warning. I was forced to resign, and when I couldn't get another job, I was forced to return."

"I missed him during that week he was away."

"Paul, why do you think she keeps coming back? There are other cafes in this so-called desirable area."

"She's been barred from the other cafes."

"I'm interested to know why you haven't had her barred."

I thought about this for a few minutes. Eventually Karen asked me another question. "Is she the only customer you treat unkindly?"

"No." The only customer I am civil to is Double E, which is her bra size as well as her drink. She is the much younger third wife of a high-profile businessman who lives around the corner, but she is having an affair with her personal trainer. We sneak out the back and have a cigarette together before she meets him in the park on Mondays, Tuesdays and Thursdays. She was a waitress before she got married so she is used to chatting in garbage disposal areas. Sometimes she'll even help me clear the tables on our way out. She says she misses the camaraderie of hospitality and wishes she could work just one night a week, but her husband would never allow it. I think this is a small price to pay for a mansion in South Yarra and a breast enlargement.

I could see that our time was almost up, so I listed all the issues I wanted to raise during next week's session, but Karen said that wouldn't be necessary; that her patient had made her point. "I think I'd like to see you alone next week Paul, at a different time."

# Eviction

There is nothing more infuriating than coming home to find Amanda Palmer lyrics scrawled all over the living room walls. After failing to remove them with sugar soap and hot water, I left a note on my flatmate's bedroom door;

Due to your recent act of vandalism, and, might I add, plagiarism, I feel I have no option but to evict you from the premises. I believe that I am well within my rights to keep your bond to repaint the living room and replace the two bottles of merlot you used to make your last batch of marinara sauce.

I hereby give you the required four weeks' notice, effective immediately.

Paul.

PS. You're fired.

I lay in bed and waited for her to find the note.

"My life is fucked!"

Then she slammed her bedroom door and presumably went to sleep.

**Policies and Procedures chapter 12, section 2 -Health and safety**

Employees acknowledge that Cafe Cinque has limited ability to control the conduct of all of its patrons, and accept the risks of injury inherent in any cafe setting. The oversized pepper grinder may be used as a weapon if you feel threatened in any way.

# Fusion

Over the past few weeks I have caught many of our regular customers eating at the new sushi bar on the corner. I understand the need for variety in their diet, and have made a few small changes to our menu to lure them back to Cafe Cinque. The following ad was placed on Seek this morning;

**Wanted – Spring Roll Technician for Italian Style, European Feel, Fusion Cafe/ Restaurant/Bar. Must look authentic.**

# Theft

I came home to an empty kitchen. My flatmate had vacated the premises and taken most of my belongings with her, including my futon. I made a temporary bed from towels and blankets and used my jacket as a pillow, cursing the Readings notice board and my refusal to interview more people when the room was available.

**Wanted – Mature-minded person to share older-style apartment with published writer. Must have own futon. No lesbians.**

This morning the new girl presented me with a list of demands, which included "pay for services rendered" and a promotion. I explained that she wasn't eligible for a promotion until she passed her twelve month probationary period, and that according to Policies and Procedures, she actually owed us money:

> **Policies and Procedures chapter 12, section 4 Promotions**
>
> Cafe Cinque promotes staff members and grants pay rises to employees who demonstrate an exceptional standard of customer service and a strong work ethic. Those employees who fail to maintain high standards may be penalised. (See chapter 13, section 7 of this manual – Penalties)

# Romance is dead

It took me all morning to work out what was different today; we had the same customers (except Skinny Latte, who left me a note to say she is boycotting the café until further notice) and the same music, but the cafe seemed less lively than usual. During lunch I finally realised that the new girl had stopped dancing. She stood in front of table 4 staring at the wall while the customer read the specials board. I heard him order something, I saw her write it in her notebook, but then she remained standing in the same spot. I came out from behind the machine and gently pushed her in the direction of the kitchen, where she placed the docket on the bench. I made two mochas and rang the bell. She walked like a normal person to the bench, picked up the coffees, but remained standing in front of the counter. I came out from behind the machine again and gently moved her around to face table two, then prodded her. She walked to table two, placed the coffees on the table and remained standing until I gently steered her towards the office and told her to take a seat.

"You're more useless than usual. Is something wrong?"

"No." But she was on the verge of tears.

"Forget for a moment that I am your superior. Pretend that I am a well-meaning friend."

"We broke up." Then she started crying and we were out of napkins so I had to give her a receipt roll to wipe her nose on.

Between sobs she told me some convoluted story about visiting No Choc in the hospital. He was asleep when she arrived, so she tidied up his things; skate magazines, get well cards, a Jay-Z biography and a sheet of paper with the following words scrawled on it; hearse, verse, reverse, terse, purse, diverse and curse. She knew immediately that he was writing a new song about a nurse. When he woke up she confronted him about it and he confessed to meeting someone else, explaining, "Nothing rhymes with *waitress.*"

Although I have strict rules about fraternising with the kitchen staff, I have let my spare room to the new spring roll technician, a 32-year-old virgin from Madras, figuring that he was probably born in a slum and would be more than happy to pay top dollar to live in a cold, dark, damp flat in East Coburg. When he came to inspect the room he asked if I knew any loose women. On his first night I politely explained that under no circumstances do I share or lend toiletries, condiments or cleaning products, unless he is cleaning communal areas such as the hallway and the living room. Utility bills are split according to how much time we spend at home, and that he must fill in a time sheet whenever he enters or exits the flat. He is saving to bring the rest of his family to Australia and I have made it very clear that they are not to stay here. He cooks most evenings, and I wait until he is asleep then help myself to leftovers. I can never remember his name so I just call him Pappadum. He doesn't seem to mind.

> **Breakfast special** – Trail mix muffins. May contain traces of chorizo.

The familiar beep of a refrigerated truck reversing into the loading zone is one of the few things that can bring my manager out of the office. She flirts shamelessly with the delivery men. The young ones are afraid of her and prefer to deal with me, but the crusty old men in

King Gees love her.

"How is ya?" she asks, leaning seductively against my Gaggia.

"Better now," they reply and give us someone else's vegetables or an extra crate of beer. She makes them cups of tea and they stand by the counter discussing the weather or the footy. Our small goods supplier is especially taken with her. He used to come in fortnightly, but now he comes in every day, even though we stopped paying our bills months ago. Sometimes he will stay for a chat, but today he was busy so he left the engine running while he dropped off a gift. "A little something to remind you of me," he said, and handed her a giant salami.

Pappadum doesn't spend a lot of time in the apartment, which makes him the perfect flatmate. When he isn't working, he's at William Angliss, where he is studying for a diploma in Hospitality Management. While tidying his room this evening, I found a collage he had made of all the things he hopes to achieve in Australia; a Tudor-style mansion, a Mercedes convertible, an Indian restaurant and Rebecca Gibney.

When he got home I asked him if he'd like to watch Packed to the Rafters with me, but he had a Skype appointment with his mother. I went to my room and started my own aspirational collage; a vintage Gaggia, an art deco apartment, a Pulitzer Prize and Anton Enis.

**Note to customers** Please note that the fat-free muffins are free of fat, not free of charge.

Skinny Latte came into the cafe today after a lengthy absence. She didn't explain why she was back, but I can safely assume she has been barred from wherever she discovered 'real chai', which she asked to be made with skinny milk. "It's called *skinny* milk, not *make me skinny* milk," I informed her as I placed her drink on the table. She chose to ignore me. She obviously acquired a fetish for Indian men during the boycott; as Pappadum made his way to the garbage disposal area she stopped him and told him he had beautiful eyes. She wrote her number on a napkin and tucked it into his apron.

Pappadum spent the rest of the day asking the dish pig how to pleasure a woman. Before closing, he sent her a text, "I like shave pussy!", so that she would know he had a preference and was therefore not a virgin. Amazingly, she wrote back with her address, telling him to be there at 7pm. He then sent a second text, "Get ready for the Indian cobra!", doused himself in Windex and made his way to Glen Iris.

My manager's therapist suggested she find a creative outlet outside of work. She has joined the Ferntree Gully Community Players and is preparing for her role in their upcoming production, *Agnes of God*. I am free to run front of house as I please again, as she spends most of her time in the office learning her lines.

At the audition they asked her if she would be willing to sell refreshments in the foyer before and after each show. She said this was no problem, and was offered the part immediately. She also has to provide her own costume.

When I asked her about rehearsals she replied "Couldn't organise a fuck in a brothel, Paul." I know this pleases her, as she can take over. She likes to organise things. The cafe is a lost cause, but the theatre presents new possibilities. She has spent hours drawing up rosters, organising group bookings for local businesses and writing press releases. We don't usually allow advertising in the cafe but every available surface is covered with flyers for *Agnes of God*.

"Don't you think you should wait until after opening night before inviting people you know? This is supposed to be therapeutic." I could see this going terribly wrong and was secretly excited about it, until she told me that she intends to perform sober.

This is not the first time my manager has attempted to stop drinking. I have a small scar on the back of my neck from the previous time, and a bald patch on the side of my head from the time before that. When I suggested that going cold turkey is not for everyone, she assured me that this time will be different, because she finally has a reason to stop drinking. I urged her to join the local AA group, but she insisted that her hectic rehearsal schedule leaves her little time for anything else. I removed all sharp objects from the office and will wear my bike helmet indoors for the next few days.

**Policies and Procedures, chapter 22, section 8 – Physical violence**

Anyone caught resorting to acts of physical violence to resolve conflict or prove a point will be fired immediately and may face criminal charges. We also ask that you avoid activities which may incite violence in others. Previous examples of entrapment include but are not exclusive to:

☐ Taking a lunch break longer than the time permitted, especially on weekends

☐ Giving incorrect, incomplete or illegible orders to the kitchen and/or barista

☐ Taking the customer's side during a disagreement over standard of service, quality and/or cost of food and/or beverage

☐ Stacking dirty dishes incorrectly (please refer to chapter 11, section 5 – Dirty dishes)

☐ Leaning on the Gaggia

The owner came in this morning to raid the safe but it was empty. He looked at me suspiciously.

"Where's the money?"

"There isn't any." I produced a week's worth of Z reports and explained that after paying the power bill, the bread supplier, the juice guy, the milk supplier and the butcher we had made an average of thirty dollars a day. I never put the first $120 through the till, as I pay myself cash at the end of each shift.

"Don't pay any more suppliers." He helped himself to some coins from the petty cash drawer and left for an important meeting in the city.

# Consultant

We have acquired the services of a management consultant who has promised to "optimise performance levels across the board" and put the cafe back in the black. This person has never owned or worked in a cafe, but he charges $120 an hour, so I assume he knows what he's doing. He has a temporary office on table 14; laptop, iPad, mobile phone, headset. He sent me a Google invite to chat with him after lunch. As I approached his table he shook my hand and motioned for me to sit down.

"What do you think this establishment needs, Paul?"

"We need more straws." Actually, I'm pretty sure we have lots of straws but retrieving them from the store room involves moving all the spare copies of the Policies and Procedures manual and I couldn't be bothered.

"Buy more straws, Paul."

He looked into my eyes, holding the stare for longer than was comfortable. I thought that I had missed some hidden meaning in his statement, but it turns out he was just trying to empower me with the ability to make firm decisions. After lunch I received another Google invite to discuss the progress of the buying of the straws.

"How are we going with the straws Paul?"

"I haven't had a chance to call the supplier."

"Let's escalate this to the next level."

We spent the rest of the afternoon drafting a request for tender, which will be sent to all suppliers of straws in Victoria. Under 'desired outcomes' I wrote; *Ease of drinking for stakeholders of Cafe Cinque cafe/restaurant/bar.* When we were done we had 34 pages, including an introduction to Cafe Cinque, an explanation of the current methods for purchasing straws, specifications and constraints, ordering and delivery requirements, and two chapters devoted to relationship management. We also included an implementation timetable and a glossary.

After extensive online research I have come to the conclusion that I have a vitamin B deficiency. Apparently this is quite common amongst hospitality workers who start early and finish late. I'm taking vitamin B supplements, and spend my lunch break in the park across the road. "Those milk jugs are not to leave the premises Paul. Someone else can make coffee while you have your lunch. Get over yourself." Usually I would ignore my manager, but I am avoiding conflict while she is not drinking. I use a pair of binoculars from the lost property basket to keep an eye on the Gaggia. If anyone dares to use it while I'm away I call the café from my mobile and talk them through the correct way to make a coffee. Then I make them take a photo with their phone and send it to me for approval. Yesterday the new girl used chocolate syrup to put smiley faces on three cappuccinos. I had to cut my break short to issue her with a written warning.

**Policies and procedures, chapter 6 section 3 – Response Management**

As a member of this team, you will often be the bearer of bad news for customers wanting to secure a certain table, order something temporarily unavailable or requiring special treatment. When denying certain requests, you may use the following phrases to ensure that the customer remains calm:

☐   "I regret to inform you"

☐   "Unfortunately"

☐   "Due to circumstances beyond my control"

It is important that the customer does not become agitated until they have paid their bill.

# End of tenancy

I came home last night to find Pappadum and Skinny Latte practicing tantric sex on my living room floor. They ignored me as I ran to my room, where I spent the rest of the evening curled up on my bed in foetal position, hands over my ears. I emerged this morning to find the following note on the fridge; *Paul! I am love! I live with her. God luck to you mate!*

I helped myself to some left over curry and posted the following ad on Gumtree:

**Wanted. Mature-minded person to share older-style flat with writer. No lesbians. No Indians.**

We have only received two responses to our Request for Tender. The consultant created a spreadsheet to compare price, delivery timeframes, and their differing levels of customer support. It turns out that both suppliers' straws are exactly the same, as are their prices, so our decision was based on environmental impact; by engaging the company closer to the cafe, we are minimising our carbon footprint. We sent the successful supplier a letter of congratulations and placed an order for 3000 long straws, to be delivered by end of business Monday.

# Moniker

Most customers know that I do not converse with the general public before 9am. Some, however, insist on greeting me when they order coffee.

"Mornin' Sandy."

This is a nickname I earned when someone had changed the settings on the grinder during my break and I refused to make coffee until they were fired. The manager apologised for my behaviour to the long line of customers that had formed while I stood there, explaining, "Paul has sand in his vagina."

Obviously, anyone who dares to call me Sandy risks an over-extracted coffee. I am also referred to as the rude one, the tall one, the unhappy one and the one with a bug up his arse about soy milk. I know that some customers get off on my so-called bad behaviour; often they will provoke me in order to be abused. On such occasions I refuse to react. I am not a performing monkey.

My manager has taken two weeks' leave without pay to prepare for opening night. Before she left, she changed the code to the safe to prevent me from using the cafe's money on 'unnecessary items'. She forgot, however, to change the password on the office computer, so I logged into her RSVP account and updated her profile: 'Ungrateful old boiler seeks man with low expectations for companionship and occasional grope. Must have own paddle.'

My manager has been on RSVP for years, but she is not looking for a life partner. She just wants to keep her options open in case the owner refuses to leave his wife. Usually she arranges to meet potential dates at the cafe, where she feels safe. On these days she pays more attention to her make-up and wears Spanx under her work pants. If she likes the way they look she will sit down with them, if she doesn't, she simply keeps working. She bears no resemblance to her profile photo, which was taken in 1995, so they just assume they've been stood up. You can always tell how lonely someone is by how long they are prepared to wait. One man stayed the entire day. Sometimes she will ask me what I think but I withhold judgement until they have placed their coffee order; short blacks mean candlelit dinners at high-end restaurants and long weekends on the Mornington Peninsula, cappuccinos with extra froth mean sausages and coleslaw at the San Remo caravan park on Phillip Island. A lot of men over seventy include photos of a newly acquired caravan in their profile, named after a recently deceased spouse.

Every now and then, when the owner has cancelled yet another weekend away, she will agree to a date with one of these men. They never work out – men in her age group usually want much younger women, and the ones willing to settle for someone older have omitted important information from their own profiles; 'likes long walks on the beach' rarely includes the fact that their arthritis prevents them from walking on sand, and 'appreciates good wine' never includes the fact that if they have more than one glass, they suffer from gout.

**Policies and Procedures Chapter 12, Section 3 – Staff discounts**

Please be aware that staff discounts are a privilege, not a right. Only those employees who have passed their mandatory twelve-month probationary period may apply for discounted meals. Approved staff are entitled to 3% off all cooked meals and 5% off all sandwiches (please note a toasted sandwich constitutes a cooked meal.) These discounts are granted at management's discretion and are subject to change without notice.

Staff are permitted one free coffee per shift, but extras such as soy milk, decaf or artificial sweetener incur a charge of fifty cents. Staff meals are to be eaten in low priority seating or in the garbage disposal area at the rear of the premises.

Under no circumstances are discounts to be given to relatives, friends or significant others.

Under no circumstances are discounts to be offered to customers as compensation for poor service or bad food.

Our new straws arrived today, but they are too long. I sent a Google invite to the consultant for an emergency meeting after lunch.

"How is everything going, Paul?"

"The new straws are too long."

The new girl suggested cutting the long straws in half, but the consultant and I agreed that we should draft an RFT for taller glasses.

# Opening night

(or the beginning and end of my manager's brief foray into amateur theatre)

Scene: the dilapidated stage of the Ferntree Gully Players Theatre.

A dramatic score plays over a crackling sound system.

The score ends, and is repeated.

Faint movement from behind the faded velvet curtains.

The sound of someone being dragged onto the stage against their will.

Music stops abruptly.

Curtain rises to reveal Manager, horrified.

Silence.

Approximately twelve minutes of silence.

The music starts again and the curtain drops.

The end.

I spent the rest of the evening trying to coax her out of the dressing room. The director, a recent VCA graduate, insisted the show continue, as he had invited two people from the Melbourne Theatre Company. The manager's lines were delivered by the director's mother from behind the curtain. Halfway through act three she walked onto the stage to tell her son, "You should have done a musical, Gary. Everyone likes musicals."

**Foreign coins in tip jar** Customers please be advised that no one currently employed at Café Cinque is planning a trip to New Zealand, Fiji or the Dominican Republic.

**Foreign coins in register** Staff please be advised that we only accept Australian currency at Café Cinque. Anyone caught taking foreign currency from customers will be paid with said currency.

I have spent all morning convincing my manager that although she did not actually perform in *Agnes of God*, her brave attempt to pursue an interest outside of hospitality has inspired me to do the same and that she should be proud of herself. We agree that the journey is more important than the destination. Usually, I would just gloat and remind her of her shortcomings at every given opportunity, but since she stopped drinking she looks great and there is a small part of me that wants her to be happy. Not too happy though – not until I'm happy. We celebrate her success with two bottles of Sav Blanc and some vodka.

---

**Urbanspoon** I order the coffee. You make the coffee. You do not look at me disapprovingly and say 'no judgement' as you pass it over the counter. See below for dictionary definition of 'barista'. GourmetDi.

---

The industry definition of barista is, of course, slightly different: one who hides behind the coffee machine in order to avoid the less glamourous chores such as waiting on customers, running food and wiping tables. If asked to do any of the above, the barista will respond with: "I can't leave the coffee machine", "I have to adjust the grind," or simply "I'm the *barista*."


There is a problem with the taller glasses. They are only slightly smaller than our water jugs, which have to be refilled every time a stakeholder gets a glass of water. This water is free, so the constant refilling of jugs is a complete waste of resources, especially as we are understaffed while the manager is in rehearsal. The consultant said this will take a while to sort out, and created a spreadsheet so we can compare our options. I suggested purchasing much bigger water jugs. The consultant pointed out that the lifting of large jugs may be an occupational health and safety issue, so the cost of training staff and customers in the proper way to pour water must be included in this option. The new girl suggested providing each customer with a straw, which they can use to drink straight from the jugs.

The consultant is permitted to eat whatever he wants while working at the cafe. This morning he ordered the organic muesli with organic seasonal fruit, and when he hadn't received it by lunch time, he sent me a Google invite to discuss "adjusting customer expectations around delivery timeframes of certain menu items."

He asked me to sign off on a Time in Motion study. He placed an order for fully certified free range scrambled eggs on hand sliced, toasted organic sourdough and brought the Time in Motion spreadsheet up on his computer screen.

| *Time to order* | | |
| --- | --- | --- |
| *Time to start cooking* | | |
| *Time to plate up* | | |
| *Time to garnish* | | |
| *Time to run out* | | |

This is to help us identify Single Point Sensitivity (SPS). He sent me a Google invite to discuss the results. It is unclear at which point the delivery time frame is prolonged; all aspects of service delivery are slow. I called an emergency meeting, and by end of business we came to the conclusion that delivery time frames can only be improved if customers serve themselves.

I closed the café while the consultant and I devised a list of Key Performance Indicators that will help us determine how to streamline service. The chef has made it very clear that under no circumstances am I to interfere with the kitchen, so for now we have decided to focus on the processing area front-of-house. During lunch, customers may order food which is on display in the pastry cabinet; home-made quiche, house-made pies, individually prepared pastries and gourmet focaccias. If it's busy, table service is suspended and all orders must be placed at the counter. This helps alleviate the pressure of the lunch time rush as most customers resent having to line up and leave. The new girl is stationed between the pastry cabinet and the microwaves; she is responsible for retrieving dockets from the machine next to the register, re-heating food and placing it on the bench for the other wait staff to run to the tables. If she doesn't remove the dockets as soon as they appear, they pile up, creating what is referred to in the industry as a 'clusterfuck'.

The consultant monitored this area yesterday and discovered that the new girl's solution to a clusterfuck was to throw the dockets away and plead ignorance when a customer inquired about their lunch. The current wait time for a home-made quiche with seasonal side salad is

47 minutes. The consultant phoned me from the terrazzo, where he had set up office during a rare sunny spell.

"Let's do an action plan and then we will put procedures into place for a meeting to discuss best practices regarding the lunch rush."

I suggested a bain-marie, which would allow customers to serve themselves, thus removing the need for microwaves and the new girl. The consultant created a new spreadsheet to determine the cost of replacing microwaves with a bain-marie. I called Cedar Hospitality and inquired about purchasing one.

The bain-marie was delivered this morning but we forgot to measure the processing area, and it blocks access to the drinks fridge, the kitchen and the office. The consultant called an emergency meeting and we decided to hire a new team member, whose sole responsibility is to retrieve the dockets from the machine next to the register and place them along the top of the pastry cabinet so the new girl can focus on re-heating food and garnishing plates. The cost of this new person is $14 an hour, but having one staff member dedicated to the retrieval and placement of dockets should save exactly six seconds per order, translating into a cost saving of 2 cents per order, which is estimated to be a saving of $70 in the first year and $700 over the next four years. It is important not to discount the fact that a shorter wait will also result in improved customer well-being which contributes to the overall atmosphere of the cafe, which is priceless.

The New new girl got confused and instead if placing the dockets left to right along the pastry cabinet, she placed them right to left, so that the new girl re-heated the meals in the wrong order. As a result, some customers received their lunch within four minutes of ordering, and some waited an hour and a half.

I fired the New new girl and put the microwaves in the store room.

**Note to Staff** Tables 6-21 have been removed to make room for a salad bar for stakeholders who wish to eat low on the food chain. As part of our in-house Emissions Trading Scheme, a ten percent surcharge applies to cooked meals, and a ten percent discount offered to any customers willing to help plant drought-tolerant plants on the terrazzo.

I arrived to work this morning to find that someone had stolen all of the drought-resistant plants from the terrazzo. I took a taxi to St Kilda Rd police station and filed a report, and by the time I got back an angry mob had gathered at the front door, demanding to be let in. The coffee machine had been turned off overnight, so after reporting the cleaners to immigration, as this is not the first time they have fiddled with the Gaggia, I announced that there would be no coffee for at least forty minutes.

The chef had called in sick, so I was forced to sell yesterday's muffins, which were rock-hard and had to be re-heated in the microwave. No one had bothered to clean the microwaves the night before, so most of the muffins were returned with complaints that they tasted of yesterday's chorizo soup. The ladies' toilet was blocked again but we couldn't afford a plumber so I pulled up my sleeves and asked the new girl to pass me the plunger. She disappeared out the back and returned with a coffee plunger. I grabbed the other one from behind the toilet and held both plungers in the air for her to see.

"This one unblocks the toilet. This one brews coffee."

"Oh, right."

"If you forget, a simple clue is that one is usually kept next to the toilet, and the other is behind the counter, with the coffee beans."

"Roger that."

"It's not hard."

"It's just that usually when you ask me to get you something, it's for coffee."

"But we are standing in the ladies' toilet. I don't make coffee in the ladies' toilet. That would be a serious health hazard."

I ordered the new girl to re-read chapter 17, section 3 of the manual; Occupational Health and Safety, and closed the cafe while I went to the hospital for a tetanus shot. When I returned I remembered that we had a booking for the local mother's group and that they had organised a set menu and paid in advance for a two-course meal and a glass of wine each. I ordered pizzas from down the road and forged my manager's signature on a cheque, hoping they wouldn't cash it for at least a week. We had three catering orders which I outsourced to 7Eleven. A woman found a hair in her quiche and when I joked that it was organic, she bit me. I closed the cafe again but was refused a second tetanus shot so I doused myself in Dettol, staining my shirt.

Flat White came into the cafe towards closing time, ordered a beer and sat at table four. He watched me from behind the *Herald Sun* as I back washed the Gaggia, soaked the group handles and the steam wands, cleaned out the pastry cabinet, cashed off the till, stacked the chairs and swept the floor. He studied the lunch menu as I mopped around him. I turned the music up. I switched the lights off. I stood in the dark, furious, and waited for him to leave.

He asked me if I'd had a busy day. I replied that I'd had a **long** day. This man couldn't take a hint. I didn't have the energy to use force. Then he asked me if I liked long walks down dark laneways with large bins. I ignored him and considered calling the police. He cleared his throat nervously and asked if I'd like to get a drink and something to eat. With him.

I pretended I had to make a phone call and hid in the office. I made a list of all the reasons he would want have a drink and something to eat with me, and then I made a list of the pros and cons of having a drink and something to eat with him. It was a difficult decision, but in the end, the fact that I was lonely far outweighed the possibility that he was a serial rapist, so I freshened up as best I could in the staff toilet and we trammed it into the city. We sat towards the back, facing several posters urging young males to get checked regularly for STDs.

"Have you ever had an STD?" Not the best conversation starter but I was nervous.

"No."

"Either have I."

I spent the rest of the trip studying a Yarra Trams pamphlet.

In a tiny bar at the end of Meyers Place, Flat White asked me about my long day and I told him about the muffins, the hairy quiche, the blocked toilet and the stolen plants. I realised all of my grievances sounded petty when spoken out loud. I was embarrassed and wanted to go home, but he seemed genuinely interested and I found myself talking for most of the night.

I talked while the bar staff washed glasses and re-stocked the drinks fridge. I talked while they cashed off the till, stacked the chairs and swept under our feet. I talked as they turned the music up. I talked while they switched the lights off and coughed loudly. Maybe it was the wine, or the fact that we were now seated in the dark, but for the first time in my life I spoke honestly and openly. I admitted I wanted to be a writer, but I was afraid. I was afraid that I was no good, that all I could do was make coffee and that I would be making it for the rest of my life. And he listened. He listened as I admitted that I spoke down to staff members who would eventually make something of their lives and leave Cafe Cinque, but that I would grow old behind the Gaggia. That I would probably die behind it. That I abused customers to make myself feel better. But I didn't feel better. I felt duped and trapped and I was exhausted.

"Why don't you write about your job? Why don't you write about your feelings?"

I considered this as we were forcibly removed from the bar.

On the way home I realised that I hadn't asked him anything about himself, and I was overcome with a sudden urge to know everything about him. I couldn't sleep, I just lay in bed and watched the clock until it was time to get up and go to work, where he would be waiting for me to open up.

# Morning after

I arrived to work earlier than usual but there was no sign of him. At 7.33 I went to his tram stop, but he wasn't there either. Throughout the day, customers returned their coffees, complaining that they hadn't ordered flat whites. My manager asked me if I was okay. I lied and told her I was sick. I went home early and made a list of all the things I may have said to offend him, knowing full well that I simply talked about myself too much, and that I would probably never see him again.

The consultant has been offered a more lucrative contract with a not-for-profit organisation seeking to streamline their donations process. On his last day with us, he submitted a brief report stating that Cafe Cinque is approaching "end of life" and an invoice for $10,000 plus GST. I put them on the manager's desk with the other unpaid bills. When an irate customer inquired about the progress of her omelette, which she had ordered before noon, I replied "If we haven't resolved it back to you, we probably haven't actioned it yet." Then I closed the café to attend to some important paperwork. Not to be out done by the dish pig, who claims to have carpel tunnel syndrome from handling large bunches of teaspoons, I am seeking compensation for second-degree burns, sustained after spending a total of forty-five minutes trying to light the portable gas heaters on the footpath with a cigarette lighter.

**WRITE THE NEXT GREAT AUSTRALIAN NOVEL!**

This six-week course will teach you the basic skills needed to create characters and plot and evoke empathy in your readers. Course details available on the CAE website.

I decided I had nothing to lose and registered for the class. I paid for it with money from the till and filed the receipt under 'Self Improvement'.

# Writing class

I am the only person under thirty in a room full of middle aged women, many of whom I recognise from the wine appreciation course I took earlier in the year. We take turns telling the class what we hope to achieve here. Most intend to write their memoirs. The teacher says it helps to write what you know. She is a published author, but must teach these classes to make ends meet. She advises us not to write expecting to make lots of money; that for every Stieg Larsson there are millions of writers waiting tables, or making coffee. Instantly I feel more like a writer. When she asks if any of us have been published, I produce all three volumes of the Policies and Procedures manual.

We are given a short writing exercise. The teacher gives us the first line: 'I remember,' and flicks through a magazine as we try to remember something worth writing about. I have nothing. I put my head down and pretend to write. After fifteen minutes the teacher asks if anyone would like to share their work with the class. A woman in red Birkenstocks raises her hand.

"I remember I was not wanted ...."

She reads in a steady voice and by the end everyone is teary-eyed but my life is more tragic than hers. Yes, she was given up for adoption, abused by nuns at the orphanage, and sold into sex slavery, but now she works in Marketing and earns a decent salary. She doesn't exist on a steady diet of teriyaki chicken stolen from the fridge at work; she doesn't have to share a run-down flat with a series of deadshits; she can probably afford to live alone. I won't be outdone by this woman. The teacher admits that there is a market for misery memoirs, and suddenly I know what my book will be about.

It will be about me.

I am not just scribbling about my job; I am furthering a genre.

I announce to the class that I too am writing my memoir, *The Gaggia from Behind*. No one in the class knows what a Gaggia is, so I consider other titles.

Now, if a customer says something particularly stupid, I ask them to repeat it and record it word for word in my Moleskine. The new girl has agreed to record all of her interactions with customers on her phone so I can transcribe them at the end of the day. The manager is less accommodating. "Paul, remove that recording device from my face or I will ram it so far up your arse you will wish you were never born. DO NOT be an arsehole today."

Obviously, when she is here it is almost impossible to find time to write. She went home early this afternoon so I took an extended break to work on chapter 4 and whether or not I should refer to myself in the third person. On days when I don't want to be found I hide in the storeroom. It's cramped and I can't stand upright, so I squat between metal shelves stacked with old crockery, a laundry basket full of wet tea towels and musty aprons, and 300 copies of the Policies and Procedures manual. I sipped my wine and tried to drown out the noises of the cafe. The music was muffled but I could still hear the clanging of cutlery and plates being thrown into the sink. Someone knocked on the door but I ignored it. A note was slipped through the crack: *Do we have any spare napkins in there?* I replied *no* and slid it back. When my legs began to ache from squatting I attempted to sit down and got stuck between the door and the shelves. I considered using olive oil to grease my arms but couldn't reach the spare tins from where I was. When I had been there for forty minutes, ten minutes over the time permitted for my lunch break, no one came to get me. I tried not to think about the guy who cut his own arm off to avoid dying pinned under a rock. I cried for help and eventually the new girl opened the door but she couldn't open it all the way because I was lodged behind it. She called the dish pig, who broke the door down, kicking me in the head.

I returned to the Gaggia to find the new girl had arranged the dockets neatly along the top of the machine and across the bench. The last one read; *Iced chocolate. No ice. No chocolate.*

> **Note to customers – air conditioning**
> As our air conditioning unit can only be reached while standing on
> a chair, any adjustment made by someone who is not an employee
> of Cafe Cinque becomes a serious occupational health and safety
> issue. The air conditioning must remain at 3 degrees Celsius until our
> refrigeration issues are resolved. We appreciate your understanding in
> this matter.

Perfectly good reasons a certain customer has not come into the
cafe for almost a week:

- He is dead
- A member of his family is dead
- He is in a critical condition after surviving a terrible accident.
  This condition prevents him from communicating to medical
  staff his desire to contact me
- He knows I lied about never having an STD.

I scoured the papers for recent accidents involving men in their
early thirties. I tried using the manager's credit card to place an ad
in the Financial Review, but she had exceeded her limit having her
varicose veins stripped.

> **Urbanspoon** When I call you and you make the mistake of answering
> DO NOT pretend there is a problem with the connection and hang up
> on me. I gave you life! GourmetDi.

My mother insisted I have dinner with her tonight. I meet her at
the Green Dragon, where we have been eating the same three dishes
since before I started school. I have had most of my birthday dinners
here. Every year I would tell my mother that I'd prefer a party, then
panic that no one would come, and settle for celebratory Mongolian
lamb and complimentary prawn crackers.

The owner greets us by name and shows us to our regular table
by the fish tank. He doesn't bother to give us menus, just replaces my
mother's chopsticks with a knife and fork and brings two glasses of
lemonade.

Half way through the lemon chicken my mother asks "Paul, have you had your heart broken again?" By "again", she is of course referring to the first time I had my heart broken. As a teenager I developed a crush on my cousin and while sleeping over he discovered my notebook containing several one act plays in which we ended up together. He called me a faggot and belted the crap out of me.

"Your problem, Paul, is that you come across as desperate. No one wants to go out with a desperado." She stops talking while a waiter puts a plate of beef in oyster sauce on the table.

"Can we just enjoy the meal?"

"You are miserable, and I think it's unprofessional to take it out on the customers." She knows this is what I have been doing because she uses the internet to spy on me.

My mother received an iPad for her birthday last year. She uses it to post reviews of Cafe Cinque on Urbanspoon, under the username GourmetDi. "Fabulous lates! Amazing cappuccinis!" This is her way of supporting me. When I don't answer my phone it is also her way of communicating with me, because she knows I log onto the site at least once a day. Recent posts include "What do you want for your birthday?" and "Have you seen my DVD remote?" Most of the reviews not written by my mother are negative, and she insists on replying to them. This morning I logged on to find:

"Perhaps we made the wrong menu choice on this occasion but the 'fusion style chorizo spring rolls' with kidney beans left us feeling unwell." by *ForkandSpoon*, to which my mother replied, " Kidney beans are an excellent source of vitamin B!! Perhaps your aversion to fusion style food is rooted in xenophobia!"

When she's annoyed with me she writes bad reviews, such as "The barista has an exaggerated sense of his own fabulousness but is not too big for a smack." Technically she is using a very public forum to threaten physical violence. But I can't take legal action until I retrieve my belongings from her garage.

I imagine introducing her to Flat White, and decide it is easier to remain single. If he ever bothered to come back to Cafe Cinque and we ended up together, eventually I would have to bring him here. My mother would introduce him to the waiters as my "special friend," then have a stress about the dim sims; there are four per serve and usually my mother and I have one each and my sister has two. Should we order extra, or would my sister be okay with just one? The waiters would bring him a menu but my mother would tell him that we always order the same thing. My family isn't one to sit around and talk during a meal. At most, we will discuss the food. My mother will attempt a conversation but it usually just ends with her recounting her day and passing judgement on the neighbours. We never leave a tip, and if my sister hasn't eaten everything my mother will ask for a doggy bag. Actually, I only remember one occasion when we required a doggy bag, the contents of which my sister finished on the way to the car.

My mother waits until the waiter comes to clear our table to say, "No boy is worth obsessing about, Paul, not even the gay ones."

In the past, a slight interest in someone has quickly led to obsession and I will stalk them for months. Stalking is easier today of course, because I can do it from the comfort of my own home. But I don't think Flat White has a Facebook account. I've tried LinkedIn, MySpace, even Grindr, but he is nowhere to be found, which makes me think I have imagined him, which makes me think I should see a doctor.

I can't ask the other staff members about Flat White because I am the only one who has served him; he leaves before the others start. Am I so lonely that I have to imagine someone to keep me company? What does it say about me that this someone is a customer who I abuse and ignore?

I had an imaginary friend between the ages of 6 and 9; his name was Victor and he was an aristocrat. One of my chores was to set the dinner table and I would set his place with the cutlery reserved for Very Special Occasions. "Paul has always had a very active imagination," my mother would say when her sisters joined us for a meal. I wasn't brave enough to criticise my mother's cooking but thought I could get away with comments like "Victor says you've overcooked the meat again and that you should get a maid."

My mother was tolerant up to a point, but when she finally decided that I was too old for an imaginary friend and that there was nothing wrong with her cooking, she said, "Victor can go fuck himself." He refused to come to dinner after that, and eventually I stopped pretending to have friends.

# Not stalking, just casually walking past Flat White's apartment a few times on the off chance that he sees me and invites me inside

He lives on the ground floor, and from what I can see from the footpath, he is neat, he doesn't have any visitors and he goes to bed around 11.30pm. He is obviously not concerned about intruders because he left his kitchen window open. He recycles glass bottles but not egg cartons. He keeps unpaid bills on the fridge. He sleeps lying on his side. Naked.

## Writing class

Tonight we are asked to think about our story's protagonist. What does he want? What obstacles does he face? How will he overcome them? What does he look like? What does he wear? How does he speak? I think about Jonathan Larson, slaving away in a second rate diner while he wrote RENT, only to die the night of the show's Off-Broadway premiere, age thirty-six. I consider myself a better-looking version of him. I make the following list:

- Physical attributes – tall, thin. Eyes – brown. Hair – amazing.
- Wants – to be significant.
- Obstacles – job.
- How to overcome obstacles – write bestseller, quit job.

Then the teacher asks us to write a scene in which our character eats breakfast but I don't eat breakfast and instead I find myself thinking about the breakfast menu, and how it needs re-writing and that I have been banned from Kinko's so must insert changes with a red pen.

On the way home I consider the countless lessons to be learned from my miserable underpaid existence. I could be a modern day Aesop. I fantasise about a not-too-distant future when my novel is on the required reading list at both the William Angliss School of Hospitality and the Cordon Bleu, and my Policies and Procedures manual is sold as a companion piece.

**Policies and Procedures chapter 14 section 2 – Needy Customers**

will attempt to waste valuable time asking questions about the menu and imparting unnecessary information about their likes, dislikes and dietary requirements. More often than not, they come from a performance background. During quiet periods you are permitted to feign interest in an upcoming show/audition/trip to LA.

**Cautionary Tale A:** A young man begins work at Cafe Cinque, eager to please both his superiors and the customers. On the afternoon of his second shift he encounters a woman who the other staff members refer to as BYO. Can he make her a cappuccino using the rice flour milk she has brought from home? She is lactose intolerant and soy milk gives her a migraine. Sure, he replies and attempts to froth what is essentially water. She thanks him and asks him to keep the carton of rice flour milk for next time. One week later she returns, and asks him to make her a sandwich using her own special gluten-free bread. Happy to oblige, he makes a tomato and lettuce sandwich, no butter. When it is time to pay, BYO claims she is entitled to a discount for providing the bread. He charges her only for the fillings. Over the next few weeks this woman demands discounts for providing her own shatter- proof cup, gluten-free muesli, dairy- free spread, sugar-free muffins, and dolphin-free tuna. On one occasion she even brings her own chair, claiming the regular chairs wreak havoc with her sciatica. The young man suspects that she is not actually allergic to anything, but is in fact mentally ill. He tries to have her committed and is branded a Bad Person. He becomes jaded. The other customers suffer. His life is ruined.

Moral of the story: There is no such thing as dolphin-free tuna.

**Cautionary Tale B:** A young man begins work at cafe Cinque, eager to please both his superiors and the customers. On the afternoon of his third shift he informs the young woman at table 6 that her voice exercises are bothering the customers on table 4. She apologises and says she is preparing for an audition. He makes the mistake of asking her about the audition and she explains it is for a television commercial which will hopefully fund her next theatre production. The young man attempts to discuss his own artistic endeavours, but discovers that this is a one-way conversation, and before he can pull himself away she has told him about her previous training, fears and aspirations, and a recent affair with a well-known director. He realises that this customer is in fact a thespian, but it is too late, he has already agreed to attend the opening of a one-woman show at La Mama. A few days later she asks him what he thought of the show. He admits he thought it was rubbish, and is branded a Bad Person. He becomes jaded. The other customers suffer. His life is ruined.

Moral of the story: There is no free parking at La Mama.

# Flat White returns

This morning I pretended not to notice Flat White waiting alone on the terrazzo. I hurried past him and locked the door behind me before he could sneak inside. I took a minute to pull myself together in the office before seasoning the machine and opening the door again.

"Good morning."

"Good morning, Paul."

I made his coffee and placed it on table four.

"How have you been?"

"Good."

I took a few deep breaths behind the pastry cabinet, went back to table four and told him as casually as I could that I was going to have a drink in the city on my way home and that if he was free he could come if he wanted, but if he wasn't free I was going to go anyway. "Sometimes I just like to go for a drink by myself, before going home, and I don't need someone to go with me but if you'd like to come that would be fine because I don't *need* to be by myself."

"Sure, that would be great."

I spent the rest of the day trying to decide if I detected sarcasm in this last statement; if by "great" he meant he would rather eat shit. I figured if he stood me up I would just start opening after 7.33am.

**Note to self** – Do not talk about yourself. Do not refer to yourself in the third person. Do not tell him about the breakdown.

The breakdown occurred just before my 28<sup>th</sup> birthday. The cafe was closed for some long overdue plumbing work and I had nothing to do for four days. I tidied the flat. I watched daytime television. I slept in. I went to a bookshop. Surrounded by other people's achievements, I suddenly felt insignificant. I found myself skimming the bios at the front of each new release, trying to determine the average age of a first-time published author. When the first few were still in their twenties, I had to sit down. I remained seated in the far corner of the shop until I was told the shop was closing. I bought another Moleskine to make myself feel better and left. On the way home I felt the world closing in on me and struggled to breathe. I went to bed and stayed there for three days. I called my mother and told her I thought I was dying. She said, "Drama is a gay man's Gatorade," which she had obviously overheard somewhere because she isn't usually that funny. She offered to make me an appointment with her shrink but I wasn't ready to discuss it with anyone else. The next day I went back to work as though nothing had happened. That was the first time I had admitted to myself that I was unhappy, but I didn't examine it too deeply. I wasn't ready, and I busied myself with other things.

# Second date - Basement bar in alleyway off laneway behind disused parking station

Three minutes into the second date it occurred to me that maybe the first date wasn't a date; no physical contact, except for when I knocked his leg under the table and apologised profusely, no exchange of phone numbers, no future plans made. As he ordered martinis at the bar, I made a mental list of possible reasons he sought my company in the first place:

- He doesn't want to pay for his coffees anymore
- He feels sorry for me
- He is in a cult and I am his latest recruit, an easy target because I am a social pariah.

Or maybe the first date *was* a date but I ruined it with my personality. Maybe he had no intention of taking it further, and he only agreed to meet me this evening because he is polite. I watched him closely for signs that he was in a hurry to leave. I made a note of how quickly he drank his martini. When he was down to the last sip I skolled mine and stood up.

"Well, I'm off, early start tomorrow."

"Okay."

I searched his face for signs of disappointment, but it was too dark to register emotion. I placed my hand on his shoulder and said, "I had a breakdown when I was twenty-eight," then left.

# Writing class

Tonight we are asked to write about our protagonist from the point of view of a pet, but I don't have a pet. Does this teacher know what she's doing? She should have made us fill out a questionnaire before we started so she knew how many of us had pets. When I voice my concerns she tells me to write about one of the customer's pets.

# Dogs

Middle-aged women this side of the river are fond of poodles, caboodles and labra-doodles. They can be found sprawled out on the terrazzo most afternoons. The floor staff must step around several of these creatures dressed in animal print coats and matching collars as they graze on side serves of bacon and fat-free cookies. Last week I tripped over a pink leather Gucci lead and twisted my ankle. I demanded that the animal be put down but its owner left a sizable tip, which I spent on cask wine and DVDs.

# Interview

A young man came into the cafe today and inquired about a part-time job. Although we have no vacancies at the moment, I granted him a brief interview so I could sit down for a few minutes. He referred to himself as a "Writer-slash-actor-slash-director-slash-waiter." He gave a little self-deprecating laugh and I disliked him immediately.

"You'll only be called upon for your waitering skills here." I gave him a copy of the Policies and Procedures Manual and asked him to read chapter 3, section 4;

> All secondary employment must take second priority to all existing job requirements at Cafe Cinque.

He said he had an audition to go to and left.

# Writing class

It is my turn to workshop, so I bring the bell from work. Some of these women like to chat and I require everyone's full attention. I ring it three times before I begin, and if I notice someone drifting off while I'm reading, I ring it again. When I am done, only one person comments:

"I have no empathy for this character, he is a twat."

Most women in the class, inspired by *Eat Pray Love*, have gone as far as Bali to find something interesting to write about. Only one managed an affair with a local. One woman couldn't afford to go overseas, so she went to Moe, where she attempted to make friends with the other people in the caravan park. So far her book is just a review of the laundry facilities.

Birkie reads four chapters devoted to her time in the orphanage. She tried to escape, was caught by the police and then beaten up by the nuns. She escaped again and tore her leg open on a barbed wire fence. While the rest of the class offers feedback, I make a list of potential titles for my novel:

Cautionary Tales of an Executive Barista

A Life of Servitude

Hospitality! A Portrait of the Artist as a Young Professional

Eat Pay Leave.

**Urbanspoon** According to their Facebook page, Café Cinque is an Italian-style, European-feel café/restaurant/bar, but fifty percent of the menu is made up of sandwich fillings, most of which are misspelt. When I tried to place an order, the waitress told me that they were experiencing unexpected delays with toasted sandwiches, and gave me a chess board. I use the term 'waitress' loosely; when my sandwich was finally ready she gave it to the man at the next table. HungryChick.

After my near-death experience in the storeroom I have decided to dictate the rest of my novel to the new girl while we are working. Four short rings in quick succession on The Bell means "Come to the Gaggia immediately. I need you to transcribe something."

She uses her phone, as she can text faster than she can write or type, then she emails the notes to me at the end of the day.

# Writing class

It is my turn to workshop again. I have considered turning my life story into a musical and bring a CD to accompany my reading. The teacher is perplexed but allows me to play it. Afterwards she suggests that I don't try too hard to tug at people's heart strings, that if I am honest and just write about my life as it occurs, people are more likely to empathise with me. She spends the rest of the class explaining that while clichés are fine in certain genres such as romance and erotic fiction, generally they are to be avoided.

# Competition

I arrived to work this morning to find *two* men seated at table 4; Flat White and a companion. He didn't read the paper; instead they talked quietly, which made eavesdropping impossible. I thought of all those romantic comedies in which the protagonist catches her love interest with another woman and shits the biscuit, only to find out much later that the woman is his sister. This man was definitely not Flat White's sister. It could have been his brother. But then, what are the chances of Flat White, who has red hair, having an Asian brother?

And if they are not related, and Flat White is attracted to this man, he couldn't possibly be attracted to me. For one thing, this man has a real job; a real job which I doubt involved wearing an apron. He carried a briefcase which matched his shoes.

I lay down on the floor and I sobbed. I didn't care who saw me or who heard me. It was cathartic. While I was down there I found the bell, the spare bell and the thermometer I had reported stolen a few months back.

Flat White found me curled up in foetal position behind the counter. "Are you okay?"

"No."

"Should I call someone?"

"No, I'll be alright in a minute."

"Is the machine on?"

I dragged myself off the floor and made his coffee.

# A writing exercise which takes into account everything I have learnt about similes, metaphors and alliteration

The cafe was a circus; a cacophony of crashing crockery and colliding customers. The new girl was drowning in a sea of incompetence.

Before last night's class ended my teacher announced, "This week I'd like you to write a scene in which your main character is blind." I vaguely remember reading Helen Keller at school and there were lots of references to shadows and light. My imagination is limited to inventing medical conditions that prevent me from coming to work on time, so this morning, after seasoning the machine but before opening the doors, I blindfolded myself with a tea towel and attempted to make a latte in complete darkness.

I have been bragging that I can make coffee with my eyes closed for years, and it is actually true. The act of making coffee comes naturally to me, like walking or breathing, and I don't need to see in order to know where everything is. Two clicks from the grinder, then I wipe the top of the group handle with the palm of my right hand. I know how much pressure to use when tamping, and press the third button from the left for a single shot. I can even tell the consistency of the milk by the sound it makes under the steam wand. I don't need a thermometer to gage the temperature; when the jug starts to burn my hand I turn the steam wand off, tap the jug on the bench and gently swirl. I start the pour near the rim of the glass and finish with a few gentle flicks of the wrist. Then I tap the glass on the bench to get rid of any bubbles that may have formed in the milk, although this is only because I am blindfolded; only an amateur would produce bubbles with their eyes open.

I kept the blindfold on and tasted the coffee: pretty good. Then I heard someone at the counter, turned suddenly and knocked myself out on the shelf above the coffee machine. The new girl who chose today of all days to arrive to work on time, suspected concussion and called a taxi. I came to as she was attempting to drag me to the door. She rode with me to the hospital. I am on a first-name basis with the nurse at reception; she rolled her eyes and told me to take a seat. A doctor finally saw me around lunchtime. Back at work I filled in an Incident report Sheet. Under *Cause of Injury* I wrote "research." For the rest of the week I have to wear an eye patch and grit my teeth each time a customer greets me with "Ahoy Matey."

I chose not to workshop this experience. Instead I wrote a few paragraphs about shadows and light. My teacher pulled me aside to discuss my book.

"I know you're writing a memoir but I strongly urge you to switch to creative non-fiction."

"What do you mean?"

"I mean, your main character needs to be less like you and more like someone who readers would like. Your character needs to be a Good Person."

"I'm a good person."

"Then I want you to write something which illustrates this."

# A short chapter which demonstrates that I can be nice to customers, which will make me more likeable and therefore more accessible to the reader:

"Can I have a coffee?"

"Yes, you can. Here it is. Have a nice day."

"Thank you."

"You're welcome."

We are supposed to workshop a total of four times each during the semester. In the first few weeks, many of the women were reluctant to read their work out loud, so I put my name down in every available space on the workshop roster. Now that they have gained confidence, they have been demanding that I give some of these up and "let someone else have a go." We also have a word limit; we can only workshop 1500 words at a time, but I often bring up to 4000 words, and I simply use a smaller font so it isn't so overwhelming for the other, less prolific students. Some women have also complained that while I demand everyone's full attention, I rarely listen to them and my written feedback is limited to "Well done you!" at the bottom of the page.

> **Note to customers RE: Melbourne Cup** Fascinators are considered an occupational safety hazard and must be removed before entering the café. Anyone with a newly acquired spray tan is forbidden to touch the furniture.

# Pitch

An editor from a well-known publishing house visits the class as a personal favour to our teacher. We each have a few minutes to talk about our work. Predictably, he is most interested in Birkie and her tale of woe, and gives her his business card. I've been rehearsing my pitch for days. I thought he'd ask for the first three chapters at least, but he just smiles and said "lovely" and moves on the next person. I ring my bell.

"Yes?"

"Why on earth wouldn't you be interested in my novel?"

"I'm looking for something I can sell. Your main character needs a point of difference. Does your barista suck other people's blood, for example? " As he explains the phenomenal success of writers such as Stephenie Meyer, I nod and pretend to take notes. I manage to fill two pages of my Moleskine, and if he had bothered to look, he would have seen that I had written "cocksucker" on every line.

I'm the first to offer Birkie feedback when she workshops later. "Listening to you read from this pile of rubbish is in itself a form of abuse." While the others comfort her, I make a list of all the things I will do with my advance when I am a published author:

- Eat on a regular basis
- Drink better wine
- Travel (further than Albury-Wodonga)
- Own matching socks
- Buy new shoes

Our teacher advises us to wait before sending our manuscript off to publishers; "First drafts are best left in a drawer for a few weeks and revised after we have had some distance from them." But I don't have a few weeks; my rent was due yesterday. I imagine a bidding war between publishers, followed by a whirlwind book tour which includes guest appearances on late night chat shows and early morning radio.

# Letter to publishers

......................................................................................

To Whom it May Concern,

Please find attached my opus, Hospitality! A portrait of the artist as a young professional. If you do not like it, pass it to someone else in the office because you are wrong. I am 33 but am willing to lie about my age so readers consider me a genius. I am reasonably good looking but feel free to have a model pose for the back cover if you think this will help to sell more copies. I am more than happy to do book tours and take part in panel discussions but would require decent coffee and an ergonomic chair. I would also appreciate it if my mother was barred from such events.

Yours Sincerely,

Paul Whelan.

......................................................................................

# Rejection

Dear Paul,

Thank you for your recent submission to our office of *Hospitality! A portrait of the artist as a young professional*. We regret to inform you that your novel isn't right for our list – we are a relatively small publishing house and have to be very selective. We wish you the best of luck finding a home for your work.

Best wishes,

The Silver Vine editorial team.

I receive several more rejections with the following observations:

"Your use of the past and present tense is confusing."

"This character is unbelievable, unlikeable and unpublishable."

"No one is going to read a book about a cafe."

"This will only sell in Melbourne."

"This will only sell in Fitzroy."

"This will never sell."

My teacher asked if the act of writing the book was enough.

No. It was not.

# Charity

The owner would like the cafe listed as a charity for tax purposes, so I have created the Cafe Cinque Foundation. Every Thursday night I offer free coffee making classes to the disadvantaged. While most of them will never be able to get a job in a cafe, for an initial outlay of $400 (the cheapest home espresso machine on the market) they can save at least three dollars a day making their coffee at home.

I've put my manuscript away and am looking at ways to raise my profile before re- submitting. My teacher suggested a blog, but no one reads blogs. Most people are too busy writing their own blogs to read other people's. I've decided to focus on what I am already good at.

**Note to customers** For the next three days I will be working to perfect the Triple Rosetta, my signature piece for the upcoming National Latte Art competition. To prevent other baristas from stealing my design, camera phones are not permitted inside the cafe until further notice. Anyone ordering a flat white or latte is required to sign a confidentiality agreement. Cafe Cinque will be closed on Saturday between 7am and 2pm while I compete. Regular updates about my progress will be posted on Twitter at @TripleRosetta#winningdesign.

Triple Rosetta is also my alias on various dating websites. It took me weeks to perfect my profile:

## Published writer seeks good-looking male for stimulating conversation. Must have tertiary education.

Only one person contacted me. He sent me a copy of his Cert IV in Hospitality Management and a photo of his abs. We met for a drink. I quoted Dostoevsky and Faulkner, but education and intelligence do not count for much in the presence of physical perfection. I knew that if I stayed I would fall in love, which means I would be jealous and insecure and prone to public displays of paranoia. I finished my drink, told him he wasn't smart enough for me, and left.

I am allowed to bring an assistant to the competition so I have asked the new girl to come with me. She has offered to tweet while I compete.

# Comp

The competition takes place at the Melbourne Exhibition Centre, which sits between the casino and the Westgate Freeway. I am one of a hundred baristas competing. After a security guard checks that my barista's holster does not contain a weapon, I am directed to my station by an enthusiastic young woman who informs me that 10%

of my entrance fee will be donated to coffee farming families in third world countries. The barista's stations are set up in rows of twenty and include a coffee machine, a bench and a small sink. The guy at the machine next to me tells me my holster is "dope." As this is being streamed live to the web, many of the competitors are wearing head sets or lapel microphones and there are two camera crews roaming around, interviewing baristas and filming them as they prepare for the event. There is a VIP section which is reserved for coffee reps, previous winners, minor celebrities and judges.

This year's MC is last year's competition winner, a barista-slash-actor who wants to be a television presenter. He wears low waisted skinny jeans and a short sleeved shirt with the collar up and the Nespresso logo stitched onto the breast pocket. After skolling an espresso he addresses the crowd: "Coffee addicts! Let's give it up for the coffee makers! This year's competition is *fierce!*"

He is considered a legend within this circle: after winning the competition he managed to re-negotiate his pay from $16.40 to $19.70 an hour. He has his own website on which he states he is passionate about coffee and the people who are passionate about coffee. He has recently acquired an agent and hopes to do the speech circuit with ex-Olympians, but for now he makes a bit of money on the side giving motivational speeches to students of the Home Barista Institute. He recently auditioned for Channel V. In his audition tape (uploaded to his website) he tells the camera he is passionate about TV and the people who are passionate about making TV. His dream is to combine his two passions and make a TV show about people who make coffee.

I do a series of stretching exercises as he explains the rules and what the judges are looking for this year. We are required to bring a photo of our design and must produce three drinks identical to the photo. We are judged on accuracy, level of difficulty and originality.

**@TripleRosetta** Will not be working on a Gaggia as the competition is sponsored by Nespresso. Have filed a complaint. #winningdesign

We are, however, able to use our own coffee. Most of the baristas have sponsors. I was unable to approach our coffee supplier about a deal as they will only communicate with the cafe through a debt collection agency. We have about two months' worth of beans stashed under the counter but I forgot to steal some at the end of my shift last night.

The MC paces the stage: "Who will triumph at this year's Latte Art throw-down, yo?"

The winner receives $200, a Toshi milk jug, and a feature article in next month's *Bean Scene* magazine. They also represent Australia in the World Latte Art Championship, held in Seattle, the holy land. Italians may have invented espresso, but the Americans invented latte art.

We are introduced to three judges: a sensory judge will evaluate our coffee based on "flavour, tactile qualities and presentation." A technical judge will assess our "accuracy and cleanliness," and the head judge oversees all aspects of our performance. A rosetta is a fairly standard design, but because I am doing three of them I hope to score points for creativity.

I do a quick lap of the hall and check out the competition. Most of the guys have facial hair and group handle tattoos. Toby's Estate, Proud Mary and Seven Seeds have stalls at the back of the hall and people line up for samples of their signature blends. Everyone speaks excitedly about crema and extraction and full-bodied aromas. A guy with a coffee plant tattoo on his neck points to my holster and says "That's next level shit, dude."

The coffee reps refuse to donate beans to someone they have never heard of, so I trade my barista's holster for 200 grams of single origin Santa Clara from the guy at the next machine. He picked the beans himself during a recent trip to Brazil, and assures me they are "intense, with definitive lemon overtones and a creamy caramel finish." He tells the camera crew that he represents the third wave of coffee makers in Australia. I want to ask him what the first and second waves are, but the crew turn to me and ask what I think it takes to produce great latte art. I tell them, "It's all in the wrist."

'Do you mean to tell us that you won't be using any tools today?'

I nod confidently, not wanting to admit that I had to trade my tools for beans. The word spreads and a crowd gathers around my station. The new girl gestures towards the bench whenever someone approaches, like a game show hostess. I hand her my iPhone and instruct her to start tweeting.

**@TripleRosetta** OMG!! So many hot guys here! #winningdesign

**@TripleRosetta** But they are all gay. #winningdesign

The MC announces that we have five minutes to recalibrate our machines. The hall is suddenly filled with the sound of metal on metal and the roar of one hundred coffee grinders. Aprons are tightened, sleeves are rolled up and benches are wiped. The new girl is supposed to make sure my station is spotless but she disappears.

**@TripleRosetta** WTF???!! No one will make me a mochaccino! #winningdesign

As the judges approach my station, I make up some spiel about the coffee I have, using all the key words: *single origin, ethically sourced, organic, Ethiopia.* I remain calm as I make my first latte. The MC is beside himself as he addresses both cameras. "This dude is off the chain! He's free pouring y'all!"

The judges write furiously in their notebooks.

**@TripleRosetta** Seriously peeps, where can I get a moccachino? #winningdesign

My second latte, identical to the first, receives a round of applause. I wipe coffee grinds from the bench as the three judges compare notes. The MC addresses the crowd that has gathered around my station.

"This man is an *artiste*. This latte is *art*. Take a photo. Hang it on your wall." A rep from Brewhouse places a hand on my shoulder. "Love your work, man. Love. Your. Work."

I imagine the headline in next month's issue of *Bean Scene*: "Paul Whelan, Off the Tools."

An entire issue of *Crèma* magazine devoted to my rise to the top. ("Many consider Paul Whelan an overnight success but he has been slaving away behind the Gaggia for years...") The cover of GQ, a guest appearance on *My Kitchen Rules* and an entire episode of *Celebrity Masterchef* devoted to latte art.

My own column in the *Epicure*. An episode of *Australian Story*. A book deal.

A pay rise.

Coffee reps give me their cards, owners of both Proud Mary and the East Brunswick Project ask for my CV. A girl with a coffee bean tattooed on her neck gives me her phone number. Someone from the Green Lotus offers to tattoo a triple rosetta on my forearm.

I have to pull myself together in the toilets.

**@TripleRosetta** Cheer up Sandy! It's just coffee! #winningdesign

In the end, my Triple Rosetta is no match for *Mona Lisa with a milk moustache*, designed by Gary from Choice Brew cafe in Auckland. Years ago, Kiwis used to come to Australia to live off the government and drink beer on Bondi Beach. Now they all want to live in Melbourne and open cafes. They have taken to coffee with a passion not seen since the French bombed the *Rainbow Warrior*.

As runner-up, I am presented with $10, a Toshi keyring and an invitation to what promises to be an 'intense' cupping session at Sensory Lab. I decline and pack up my belongings. I spend the rest of the afternoon reprimanding the new girl for her inane tweets.

Just before lunch I found the manager in the staff toilet talking to herself again.

"I am a woman in charge of her tables."

"We need you out the front, table twelve refused to pay and are threatening to call the health inspector."

"I am a woman in charge of her tables." She stood very straight, her hands clasped in front of her.

It took me a while to understand that during stressful periods the manager reverts back to her previous life, when she *was* a woman in charge of her tables, when she managed to hold down a full time job in a busy, high-end establishment while completing a BA in Performance at the VCA. She has told me on many occasions that she could have survived on tips alone and that the other waiters would watch her in awe and tell her repeatedly, "You are a woman in charge of your tables."

Experience has taught me that this is the beginning of a familiar pattern, which I have recorded and pinned to the office notice board so I know when to call in sick:

- low sales figures
- high anxiety
- excessive drinking
- self-medication
- addressing one's reflection in mirror
- verbal abuse of customer/s
- physical abuse of fellow staff member/s
- stress leave

I have decided to take the next few days off.

**Note to staff** Due to reasons I cannot disclose, Cafe Cinque can no longer purchase goods on credit. Due to other reasons I cannot disclose, the cafe is struggling to cover costs at the end of each day. The current average spend is $3.50. We have a stretch target of $27.95, which means you should be asking each and every customer if they would like a salami focaccia and a glass of merlot with their coffee. You are all required to attend a two-hour up-selling workshop on Friday evening.

**Note to staff** A few staff members have inquired about up-selling to those customers buying takeaway coffee. While we are able to sell focaccias to take away, we do not have a bottle shop licence for the wine. Please ask customers if they would like a glass of wine in emergency seating while they wait for their coffee.

**Note to staff** Due to budgetary constraints, the Cafe Cinque Christmas party will be held at Cafe Cinque. There will be no entertainment. Partners are welcome, provided they bring their own refreshments.

The thing about hospitality is that you rarely like with the people you work with. You may feel a sense of camaraderie with them during busy periods, or when you are attacked by a customer as a group, but most staff members leave before you can really get to know them and the ones who stay develop a resentment of the job and anyone they work with as a result. So when we are forced to socialise we get very drunk to avoid having to deal with each other. The night always ends badly; either with violence, an upsetting revelation or some ill-advised sex. Last night's Christmas party was no exception. We gathered in high priority around three miserable looking plates of food; curried pasta, a coleslaw and some leftover spring rolls.

The dish pig's mother arrived just after 8pm to inform him that she has lost the will to live. Although he is no longer at home, he has been coming to work in a suit for years, so that if he ever bumps into her in the street he can keep up the pretence that he works in an office. For many years she believed that he had obtained a law degree from NIDA, and that acting was something he did on the side for fun. A family friend who lives in the area spotted him in the kitchen washing dishes and called his mother. We watched in horror as she threatened to end her life and he offered to end it for her. The manager suggested a coffee to calm him down. I made him a latte, even though he is only permitted one coffee per shift and he already had one during his break. He felt the glass and slid it across the counter with a tea towel.

"Too hot."

I informed him that coffee is meant to be served between 60 and 70 degrees.

"I can't drink this."

"Philistine."

"What did you call me, racist?"

"I will not have my coffee insulted by the dish pig!"

"What have I told you about calling me the dish pig?" he asked, waving a meat cleaver in the air.

I locked myself in the ladies' toilet until the manager assured me it was safe to come out.

# Writing class

It's my turn to workshop again. The others read from their seats but I like to stand up the front. "The appliances announce themselves frequently during busy periods. The microwave door slamming, the hum of the drinks fridge, the sliding of the register drawer, the hiss of the steam wand. They help to drown out Café Del Mar volumes 1-17, each tune etched into my brain forever."

I take a sip from my water bottle and wait for them to comment before continuing. Some of the other students take sips from their water bottles to avoid having to comment. It's a competition to see who can take the longest sip.

"Sometimes I am overcome with remorse that I have wasted so much time here, pressed against the coffee machine, staring at the walls. For a while it was easy to ignore the fact that I have been here so long, because I do not plan my life beyond the next thirty minutes:

Thirty minutes to set up.

The thirty minute rush before the next person starts.

Thirty minutes till lunch.

Thirty minutes for lunch.

Thirty minutes till the afternoon slump.

Thirty minutes till closing.

Thirty minutes to get home.

Thirty minutes to unwind.

This must be what prison is like."

When I finish, everyone leaves the room to refill their water bottles.

# Armed hold up

A young man came in to the cafe today and demanded money. He pointed a syringe at the new girl who was standing by the register, and passed her a note. She had difficulty deciphering his hand writing so he read it out to her. It said "This is a hold-up." The new girl explained that she couldn't open the till unless he bought something, so he grabbed a fat-free-gluten–free-sugar-free cookie from the counter and asked if he could have it to take away. She couldn't find the cookie button on the till, as I had changed it to read "biscotti", so he put it back and asked for a toasted sandwich. Unfortunately we had run out of bread. I gave him a menu and explained that we were only serving dishes from the bottom half of the second page. He decided on a chicken and leek pie but I had just cleaned the microwaves, so asked him if he would mind heating it up when he got home. He then had the nerve to complain about the service and tried his luck at the 7Eleven up the road.

> **Note to staff** It has been brought to my attention that certain staff members are not optimising notepad usage. Please note that one menu item should take up exactly one line on a page and that unless an order includes more than fourteen menu items, it should never require more than one page of a notepad. Your assistance in this matter is greatly appreciated and will help us save money on notepads and staples.

# Money

We have received several threatening letters from suppliers demanding money in the last few days. The owner of the cafe stopped paying his bills months ago and has gone into hiding. The manager is beside herself and suspects he has run off with the girl from the laundromat across the road. His wife came into the cafe yesterday, demanding money for her next Botox treatment, but the owner had changed the code to the safe. Wanting to get in good with Barb in case she took over the business, I emptied the Oxfam tin by the register. This money is supposed to be deposited into a bank account so little Jofrey from East Timor can go to school and buy a goat for his family, but we usually just transfer it into the tips jar.

# Coffee matrix

Due to budgetary constraints, receipt rolls and notepads are temporarily unavailable. I've instructed the floor staff to use cups, saucers and teaspoons to indicate coffee orders:

**Teaspoon to the right of cup** = flat white

**Teaspoon to the right of cup, face down** = skinny flat white

**Teaspoon to the left of cup** = cappuccino

**Teaspoon the left of cup, face down** – skinny cappuccino

**Teaspoon to the left of upside down cup** = cappuccino no chocolate

**Teaspoon, face down, to the left of upside down cup** – skinny cappuccino, no chocolate

**Teaspoon, face down, to the left of upside down cup, handle facing backwards** = skinny cappuccino, no chocolate, extra froth

**Teaspoon, face down, to the left of upside down cup, handle facing backwards on two saucers** = skinny cappuccino, no chocolate, extra froth, not too hot

**Two teaspoons** = double shot

**For latte orders, use glass instead of cup.**

Complicated coffee orders which cannot be indicated using the above matrix must be politely denied.

Unless I am closing by myself, I always attend to the Gaggia first, this way by the time I have finished backwashing, the other staff have stacked the furniture and packed all the food away. Some customers will let themselves in as we are packing up, and think nothing of taking chairs off the tables and placing an order. Three women did exactly that this evening. When I stated the obvious, they assured me that they "would only be a tick, they just wanted coffee."

The manager asked me to make their three large skinny cappuccinos while she cashed up in the office.

"I'll have to re-season. I'll be at least twenty-five minutes."

She knew I was lying, as I only backwash with chemicals twice a week. "Three large skinny caps Paul. We are in no position to turn away customers." I had spent the last half-hour scrubbing the inside of the double group handle, so I had to make each coffee using the single group twice.

I ran them out myself, as the new girl was struggling with the outdoor tables and I was in a hurry to leave. I placed them on the table and made sure the women felt my disdain.

"Which one's skinny?" the fat one asked.

"They'll all skinny."

"I didn't want skinny."

Infuriating, as none of the coffees were skinny, and I had to pretend to remake one, a complete waste of three minutes. When I took it back out another woman inquired, "Is one of them decaf? I asked for decaf."

"No, you didn't."

"I meant to. I can't have coffee after 3pm, it stops me from sleeping."

I spent three minutes pretending to remake hers as well, and then she asked me to reheat it; "Don't bother remaking it, just pop it in the microwave." A classic high-maintenance request disguised as a low-maintenance remark. These always begin with "Don't bother"; "Don't bother putting it in a bag, just use the tongs to put it straight in my hand", "Don't bother with a garnish, it'll just go to waste", and my personal favourite; "Don't bother with a lid." These customers are bordering on fanatical in their dislike of take away coffee lids. They will wait for me to put a lid on their coffee before screaming "No lid! I don't need a lid!"

I placed her mug under the steam wand, and kept it there until the whole of South Yarra smelled of burnt milk.

The women eventually left when I played *On Parole* at full volume. The manager didn't bother to reprimand me; she realised the error of her ways when they asked if she could "just duck into the kitchen and make us a bowl of chips."

# Christmas

For years, the owner of the cafe has been providing Christmas cheer to the younger kids at the primary school up the road. In the first week of December, he dresses up as Santa Claus and walks around the playground handing out presents. As he was nowhere to be found this week, it was left to me to provide the Christmas cheer. With no money for gifts, I wrapped everything from Lost Property in sandwich bags, put on the Santa Suit and did my best to spread the love.

"Ho ho ho." I handed a kid some Gucci prescription glasses and an old water bottle.

"You're not Santa! You're the rude man from the cafe! You made my mum cry."

"Fuck off, you little shit. Your mother is obviously a heathen."

I try to avoid my family during Christmas. I prefer to spend the day alone in my flat with a half a dozen bottles of wine and a box of benzodiazepines. This year my mother has insisted that the whole family get together and she has already checked that the cafe will be closed, so I have no excuse not to go. She has posted countless messages on Urbanspoon about the lunch menu. She wants me to order cheese and a turkey through work but as most of our suppliers now demand cash on delivery, I am unable to pay for it. I have not seen my extended family for almost three years, when I was forced to attend my cousin's wedding in Werribee. I was asked to do a last-minute reading during the service, opened the bible to a random page and read about the whores of Babylon for a good ten minutes before anyone stopped me.

My relatives are not bad people, they are just stupid. When I was young I thought I must be adopted and made posters which I taped to all the telegraph poles in our street: "Are you my mother?" My mother tore them down and confiscated my highlighters.

My mother likes to give everyone jobs on Christmas day: set the table, cut the turkey, wash the dishes. She insists I make the coffee after lunch.

"Isn't this amazing?" she asks, pointing to her new Nestle coffee machine. "George Clooney has one. You don't have to do anything, you just put this coffee pod in here, press this button and there you have it, an expresso!"

"Espresso."

"What?"

"Espresso."

"Whatever, Paul, just make the coffee please. Aunty Edna wants a cup of chino."

My sister wants to know if I have a boyfriend. I tell her it is none of her business and she takes this as a 'no.' She is living the suburban dream in a new estate named after a non- existent body of water, an hour out of the city. She is exactly the kind of person who would come to Cafe Cinque on the weekend, if she wasn't so busy and important. She asks me when I am going to get a real job. I ask her when she is going to have her stomach stapled.

I wasn't aware we were doing Kris Kringle until this morning, when my mother called to check that I was bringing something for my sister's husband. I said of course I had something, then rode to work and helped myself to a framed print of some Guatemalans picking coffee plants on the side of a hill. My gift is from my mother: an inspirational desk calendar and a year's subscription to the Melbourne Symphony Orchestra. She buys herself a subscription every year and she hates to go alone.

I try to leave after lunch but my mother makes *the face,* so I stay. By four o'clock we are all wearing paper crepe hats and reading the lame jokes from the Christmas crackers to avoid making conversation. An old man has been staring at me from across the table for hours. When we finally make eye contact I realise it's my father. I haven't spoken to him since I was in high school.

"Your mother tells me you're a barrister."

"That's right."

"Must be interesting."

I search the table for more Christmas crackers, more jokes. In desperation I clear the table and take the dirty dishes to the kitchen. There is a big show from the women to offer assistance, but I need a moment alone.

My grandmother had also made a rare appearance. She is usually too sick or too busy planning her funeral to attend family gatherings. She has been barred from discussing coffins, eulogies and cremation this afternoon. She follows me into the kitchen and hands me a small gift, a Royal Doulton figurine I recognise from her living room.

"Gloria's nephew Graham is a poof."

My grandmother doesn't want me to die alone.

"He's about your age, and his parents are wealthy. They have that big house in Keilor East. Why don't you invite him to the funeral?"

As I stack the dishes next to the sink, I can hear Aunty Edna explain the difference between a barista and a barrister to my father.

"That's no job for a bloke."

I decide to open the cafe on Christmas Day next year, even if I have to work alone.

# New Year's resolution

* I will not ignore customers because they are ugly, fat or poorly attired.

* I will not reprimand customers for ordering their coffee incorrectly.

* I will not drink Shiraz before 10am.

# Amendments to resolution

\* I will only ignore customers who are fat and ugly.

\* I will not reprimand customers for ordering their coffee incorrectly, I will simply ignore them also.

\* I will not drink Shiraz before 10am, but I will drink Cab Sav at any time during the day, especially after dealing with fat, ugly customers who despite my best efforts, insist on ordering extra-hot, extra-frothy lattes in mugs.

# Jan 1

is the busiest day of the year and everyone is expected to work. No one does, of course. Some call in sick but most just don't bother turning up. As most of the regulars are ensconced in their holiday homes in Portsea and Sorrento, on New Year's Day we cater for those who have stumbled from the city in a drunken haze, across the river and through the park. Some fall asleep on the benches in High Priority. I don't bother enforcing the seating matrix. Others have decided not to celebrate the previous evening but are determined to see in the New Year with a champagne breakfast. We haven't stocked champagne for almost a year so I mixed Pinot Gris with mineral water. Although rostered on for 7am, the new girl arrived in a taxi just after 11, with a gaggle of girls who demanded bacon and egg rolls and strong chai lattes, to cure their hangovers. I told them that chai is not a latte as they compared hickeys and photos. One girl passed out by the kitchen door, so I dragged her behind the drinks fridge where she stayed until closing time. By 2pm Cafe Cinque resembled a King St club. The only way to deal with customers who have been drinking is to drink. I keep a large Ribena bottle filled with Cabernet behind the Gaggia for emergency purposes. If the bottle is less than half empty by lunch time, I have two double espressos and a Berocca to get me through the afternoon rush. The bottle was completely empty by lunch time, so I had two Beroccas and four double espressos and spent the rest of the afternoon in a state of mild anxiety. All orders for white coffees were refused as my hands were shaking too much to use the milk jugs.

**Incident report sheet**

**Incident no:** 456

**Time and place of incident:** 9.05 am, high priority.

**Parties involved:** Skinny Cap, Decaf Skinny Cap

**Cause of injury:** Injuries sustained during a fight over table 14. Car keys can no longer be used to reserve tables.

Ambulance called after both women contacted their lawyers and their plastic surgeons.

**Number of complimentary muffins required to placate victim:** None. Both women on the zone diet.

My manager's therapist has suggested some sort of creative outlet that doesn't involve public performance. I suggested nail artistry, but she has her heart set on jewellery design, and enrolled in a silver smithing course at NMIT. The hospitality industry is full of artistic types who work three hours a week, so they can spend the rest of their week *creating*. These people are responsible for most of the criminal activity at Cafe Cinque. My manager has fired several part time staff for not understanding the difference between "found object" and "stolen object." All of our 'position vacant' ads on Seek include 'creative people need not apply." So I was shocked when she took all of our teaspoons and assured me they will be worth more as wrist cuffs. She also promised that as soon as she makes a profit she will go to Cedar Hospitality and replace them.

She has turned the office into a studio and spends most afternoons hammering away at our teaspoons. When she showed me her first few pieces I acted amazed, as though I haven't seen wrist cuffs made from cutlery before. She offered to make me a neck piece from one of my group handles.

Because there is a glut of jewellery made from found objects in Melbourne, her applications for stalls at the Rose St, Camberwell and Suzuki Night markets were rejected. Undeterred, she removed tables 14 and 15 and set up shop in High Priority. Customers could choose between wrist cuffs fashioned from teaspoons or earrings made from forks. She offered complimentary gift wrapping and a flyer about art and sustainability, which is part of her assessment. Towards the end of the day she made a sale, and celebrated with two bottles of sparkling Moscato left over from the last mothers' group lunch.

The owner of the café made a rare appearance towards closing time and wanted to know why there was no money in the till. I explained that this week's takings had been compromised by a food truck parked across the road.

"Tacos or burgers?"

"Sliders."

"What the hell is a slider?"

"A dwarf-sized burger."

# Poet

To compete with the food truck across the road, I have employed the services of a professional spruiker. She stands by the front door between 8am and 2pm and yells into her microphone about selected menu items. During her break she told me that she is actually a performance poet, and I asked her to recite some of her work by the salad bar after lunch. I had to put this to an abrupt end when she announced to the customers that her first poem was titled "Your Cock" and was dedicated to her ex-husband.

# Sister

A few years ago, my sister attempted a reconciliation between my father and me. She would come to the cafe during her lunch break and I would lock one of the front doors, knowing she needed both open to fit through the double doorway. This also prevented other overweight customers from coming inside and breaking the chairs. My sister would pace the terrazzo gesturing for me to come outside, but I would always mime that I was too busy. I'd send a staff member outside with a notepad and instructions for her to put her concerns in writing. Eventually she gave up and even stopped calling me.

We shared a room until I was ten, when she caught me masturbating in her bed. I wasn't attracted to her, I just didn't want to mess up my own bed. She demanded her own room and my mother was forced to turn her beloved study into a third bedroom. Immediately I wished I had made such a demand earlier: her new room was bigger than mine and included a view of the neighbour's Jacuzzi. Every day after school, before she got home from one of her many extra-curricular activities, I would sneak into her room and masturbate just to spite her. She eventually caught me towards the end of high school and moved out. I haven't been able to masturbate without thinking of her since and I resent her for this. This is perhaps the reason I have never been in a steady relationship.

My sister was pacing the terrazzo when I arrived this morning. She had left her husband and needed somewhere to stay, where no one would think to look for her. I considered my options. Another transient who would steal my belongings or leave on short notice? I agreed to let her stay for the full amount of rent, thinking that I could also make a profit.

I gave her my spare key and a copy of the house rules, which had been updated since Pappadum left:

- No sharing of toiletries
- No visitors
- No tantric sex with visitors on living room floor

She was already familiar with my book lending policy and assured me that she wouldn't take my books out of the flat, that she would read them in the lounge room when I was home, and that she would use a bookmark every time. I issued her with a Book Request Form anyway.

I always thought my sister was quite well off but it turns out that most of her money is tied up in her husband's pyramid selling scheme. She made me promise not to tell my mother about the separation. We both knew what she would say: "Thank god I held on to the cutlery." When my sister got engaged my mother presented her with a 100-piece cutlery set that had been in the family for three generations. Technically it was now hers, but my mother said that she would hold onto it "in case things didn't work out." My sister accused my mother of jeopardising her marriage and their relationship has been strained ever since. Now it turns out my mother was right, and the cutlery is safe.

I came home from work to find she had cooked a three-course meal. I used to scoff my food as a kid because that was the only way to get a meal in before my sister ate everything. It took me years to slow down and chew my food: as a result I suffer from gastro-oesophageal disease. I found myself reverting to this behaviour tonight, but my sister hardly touched her food. She said she wanted to lose weight, so I offered to lend her my bike. I told her about my book and she surprised me by being encouraging. So then I told her about Flat White and she surprised me again by saying he would be mad not to go out with me.

She wanted to get drunk so we went to a bar on Sydney Rd and for the first time in my life I was not embarrassed to be seen with her. We managed to converse without an argument, and I kept her up half the night reading excerpts from my novel. She was nice enough to listen. She admitted to an affair. I always thought it would be her husband who would cheat, but three months ago she met a man in aisle six at Safeway and they have been sleeping together since. He sends her poetry. She let me read it and I didn't have the heart to tell her that it was plagiarised.

# Bonding

While tidying the flat, my sister found all of my rejection letters. She took pity on me but I assured her they only make me stronger.

We used them to line the recycling bin.

# Home Improvement

My sister has taken a few weeks off work to pull herself together. She spends most days cooking and cleaning and calling me at work with suggestions for making the flat cosier. I have agreed to a rug in the living room and the replacement of bed sheets over the windows with real curtains, provided I don't have to pay for them.

On Saturdays she meets her new beau at Safeway where they re-enact their first meeting. They approach each other from opposite ends of aisle six, and talk through what they were doing before the *thunderbolt*.

"I was looking at noodles, I couldn't decide which ones would complement a beef stir fry, and you suggested rice."

"You were standing in front of the basmati. You were wearing that plaid shirt."

"You had green curry paste in your trolley and I told you that coconut cream goes best with that particular brand."

Despite my no visitors rule, Aisle Six stays over on Saturday nights. He and my sister take turns concocting meals from ingredients bought in their favourite aisle: chicken madras, rogan josh, laksa, crispy beef stir-fry. After dinner they watch reruns of *Iron Chef*, then go to bed.

Last night I made a joke about attending a wedding at Safeway, pressed against the overstocked shelves, the bridal waltz interrupted by "Price check register two, refried beans." My sister told me, "Don't be stupid Paul, we are both married to other people."

Her husband turned up unannounced while she was out with Aisle Six. He looked like he hadn't showered or changed his clothes in weeks. He asked me how she was and I told her she seemed happy, which made him cry. He sat at the kitchen table for what felt like eternity and sobbed like a baby. In an effort to comfort him, I placed my left hand on his right shoulder, but that only made him cry more so I asked him to leave.

**Note to staff – Valentine's Day** Existing menu items should be described as 'share plates' to any customers resembling a couple this Sunday. There is a minimum order of two share plates per couple. The communal table in the middle of the cafe will be reserved for Cafe Cinque's Annual Valentine's Day Speed Dating Brunch. Customers wishing to reserve a seat at this table must apply to me in person and provide two recent colour photographs and a brief note explaining why they are single.

After a lengthy absence, No Choc chose Valentine's Day to make an appearance and the new girl finally got a glimpse of the New

Girlfriend. She wanted to hide in the office until they had gone but I explained that as a service provider, she was in a position of power. She begged me to put chocolate on his cappuccino, but I said, "We can do better than that," and told her to spit in his coffee.

It is a well-known fact that anyone who upsets a service provider will have their food or beverage adulterated in some way.

My sister's favourite form of communication is the Post-it note. She uses different colours to indicate the importance of a particular message: yellow is a standard note, pink is urgent and green means she is mad about something. Green notes usually include several exclamation marks, and some words, such as 'inconsiderate' or 'wasteful' will be underlined. This morning I counted sixteen Post-it notes in the kitchen alone; most of them green, all of them about the washing up. I like to wait until there are enough dishes to justify filling the sink, but my sister will wash a plate or a bowl as soon as she has finished with it. She doesn't believe in drip-drying either: items must be dried with one of three tea towels ("red for crockery, white for glasses and blue for cutlery!!!!!") and put away immediately. I decided not to make a scene, because we grew up in the same house and we each have our own neuroses as a result.

She refuses to hang her delicates on the communal line in the courtyard, so there are always at least six pairs of granny knickers and an oversized bra hanging over the shower curtain rail at any given time. I use them to mop the bathroom floor.

This evening I placed green Post-its on all of her delicates and put an exclamation mark on each one. She assumed I was commenting on the size of her underwear, rather than the fact that she was taking over the bathroom, and swiftly replaced all items from aisle six with Weight Watchers meals. A yellow Post-it on the fridge door explained that these meals are only to be consumed by her and that I must "catch and kill my own" from now on.

Since she was a teenager, my sister has approached weight loss with such gusto that we are all surprised when she doesn't lose anything, and sometimes manages to put weight on. When this happens, her obsessive compulsive disorder becomes more apparent, and I know that it is only a matter of time before she attempts to control every aspect of her life and most aspects of mine.

## Tuesday 6.40am

Four bottles of merlot removed from pantry to make room for three kilo tin of sugar-free powdered chai.

My sister is also obsessed with conserving energy. She switches the toaster off at the power point when she's finished with it. She switches the lights off, even when I am still in the room: "You don't need the light on to watch TV." I told her she is more like our mother than she would care to admit. She was furious, and went to her room, and I heard nothing from her for over an hour, when she came into the lounge room to inform me that I am just like our father, and then I too, was quiet.

## Tuesday 8.10pm

Byron Bay cookies missing from pantry. Have been replaced with gluten-free rice crackers. Sister uses hot water tap in kitchen to freeze me out of the shower, claiming that five minutes is more than enough time to get clean.

## Wednesday 6.10am

Cannot find shoes. After searching for twenty minutes, discover they have been placed on the back steps with a pink Post-it outlining all the germs I could bring into the flat if shoes are worn inside.

## Thursday 5.45am

Anne Geddes calendar in bathroom.

## Thursday 5.56am

New cleaning roster on fridge.

**Urbanspoon** The barista at Ginger Lee on Lygon St is such a sweetheart. I told him all about you. I really think you too could hit it off. I've invited him to dinner on Monday. DO NOT wear that shirt. You know the one. Thank me later. GourmetDi.

Needless to say, I did not go to dinner on Monday night, and I switched my phone off. Seven missed calls from my mother and a link to the dictionary definition of 'ungrateful' on Urbanspoon the next morning. Just before the lunch rush she stood in front of the coffee machine until I was forced to acknowledge her.

"What?"

"I just want you to be happy."

"I am happy."

"No, you're not, Paul, you're miserable. It's a reflection of bad parenting and I can't live with that. Promise me you'll try to be happy."

"Do you want a coffee?"

"No thank you, I'm going to Seven Seeds with Deidre. They have a syphon."

So I closed the café early and I went to Ginger Lee. The café was busy; dockets were lined up along the bench by the machine but the barista was adjusting the grind. I stood at the counter. "Dan?"

"Is that the shirt?"

He removed his apron to reveal the exact same shirt. We eyed each other warily. My mother obviously thought that I could only be happy with someone exactly like me, that I couldn't possibly find fault with someone so similar.

"This will never work."

"Tell your mum I said hi."

"You tell her."

And I left.

**Urbanspoon** You can't blame me for everything. Eventually you'll have to take responsibility for your own happiness.
Have a wonderful birthday, GourmetDi

With this in mind, I closed early again, and went back to Ginger Lee. Dan was recalibrating the machine. I rang the bell to get his attention. He didn't bother to look up, he just said, "We have table service."

"Would you like to go out on a date?" I said. So there would be no confusion about whether or not it was a date.

"Sure."

"With me?" So there would be no confusion about who the date was with.

"Sure."

I suggested Lentil as Anything, because you pay what you think your meal is worth, and I had exactly ten dollars until pay day. He offered to cook instead and gave me his address.

He lives within walking distance of his work. His apartment is much nicer than mine, which my mother refers to as povo chic. He made risotto, which we ate in the kitchen with a bottle of wine he had obviously stolen from the café. We talked shop, meaning we bitched about customers and co-workers. While he was stacking the dish washer I used the bathroom and rifled through his medicine cabinet, looking for evidence of mental illness, or other men. I found expensive aftershave and a razor. When we finished the wine he offered to drive me home. I pretended that I wasn't expecting to stay the night and gave him directions to East Coburg. When we arrived at my place I invited him inside. I was suddenly grateful for all of my sister's crap, as it lends an air of maturity to the place. I was also grateful that she was in her room, and led him to mine.

I wanted to appear to be so carefree that I could sleep with this man with the lights on. But as I unbuttoned my shirt I noticed its frayed cuffs. I thought about my bony hips and my knobbly knees, and switched the light off.

He remained clothed and I worried that I had been too eager, standing in only my underwear. He was bigger than me and I wondered if he was attracted to me because I am not masculine. Or maybe he thought I was more masculine and now he was disappointed. Or maybe he wasn't attracted to me and was wondering why I had led him to my room and taken my clothes off. I didn't want to remove my underwear until he had at least unzipped his fly. I was wearing Calvin Klein's. And when you're standing in the dark it is difficult to convey that you are wearing an outdated brand in an ironic way. I decided to kiss him and remove my undies at the same time, then subtly kick them under the bed.

"Where's my low-fat chicken parmigiana?" My sister doesn't believe in knocking first.

"In the fridge, between your low-fat tuna casserole and your low-fat chocolate mud cake."

"It's not in the fridge. Did you eat it?"

"No, I didn't eat it. Only people desperate to get down to a size 18 would eat that shit. Do you know anyone in this apartment who fits that description?"

"Are they Calvin Klein's?" Even in the dark my sister can find the one thing that will tip me over the edge. "Did you buy them recently, or have you been wearing the same undies since 1992? I knew money was tight but..."

"Get out."

"Who's your friend?"

Dan mumbled something about an early start in the morning, which is my line. He could have been turned off by my sister or my juvenile behaviour, but deep down I know it was the undies. I stood by the bed naked as he squeezed past my sister and let himself out.

"You've ruined my one chance at happiness."

"Don't be so dramatic. He's too good looking for you."

Later that night, my sister found her low-fat parma in the freezer, but refused to admit she put it there. I called my mother and revealed my sister's whereabouts.

# Chef

The chef quit this morning, claiming he could no longer work without ingredients. He hadn't been paid in over a month, so he took the Mixmaster, the meat slicer and the toaster with him, as well as our last two kilos of frozen peas. Pappadum has agreed to run the kitchen until we can find a replacement chef. He was so keen for the experience that he offered to bring his own groceries from home. Cafe Cinque is an Indian restaurant until further notice.

> **Urbanspoon** After ordering the linguini pomodoro, we were told that the pasta was no longer available but that we could have the napoli sauce on roti bread. Foodie22.

# Wednesday 7.45pm

*Bean Scene* magazines stolen from cafe removed from coffee table to make room for motivational literature purchased online. Quotes from motivational literature applied to yellow Post-its, stuck to every available surface in kitchen. There were also several pink Post-its alerting me to a house meeting which had been scheduled for 8.30pm. My sister wanted to discuss my tendency to hide the TV remote in my room so she has get off the couch to change the channel or mute the ads. Usually, by the time she has gotten off the couch, the ads are over. I suggested watching SBS.

Aisle Six lasted one week into her diet. He couldn't handle the miniscule portions of pre-packaged Steak Diane, and ended the affair, which had her heading for the pre-packaged deserts, all of them, together at the same time. When I suggested we hit the pub, she screamed "Do you have any idea how many calories are in a glass of Sav Blanc?" then spent an hour rearranging the fridge so that all of her pre-packaged meals were in alphabetical order.

Horrified that my sister was slumming it past Bell St, my mother paid a surprise visit last night. I could tell that she was trying to be supportive, but her need to gloat finally got the better of her after a

Weight Watchers chicken tikka.

"It's a good thing I held onto the cutlery."

I was forced to take cover in the bathroom as my sister threw every piece of cutlery she could find at my mother.

**Policies and Procedures chapter 13 section 5 – Espionage**

Staff are encouraged to spy on competing dining establishments in the immediate area. Coveted information includes recent changes to menu, refurbishment, average age of wait staff and the barista's annual salary.

Some of my weekday customers have been raving about a new café in North Carlton. Customers who complain if their coffee is not ready when they walk through my door had no qualms about spending a good chunk of their Saturday morning lining up outside this new place, waiting for a table. The word 'visionary' was used a number of times. I imagined this visionary walking up the Gaggia Strip, past Brunetti, Small Block, Ginger Lee, Sugardough, Poached and the Gelo Bar and saying to himself; you know what this area needs? Another café.

I closed early and went to check it out. It was your typical Melbourne café, meaning nothing matched and the service was slow. After a lengthy wait I was given a menu. It contained more adjectives than ours, and on the back was a black and white head shot of the barista, with his name across the bottom. I googled photographers while I waited for my coffee to arrive.

**Note to staff** Due to budgetary constraints, portion control guidelines now include toilet paper. One sheet per customer per visit (supplied on request with presentation of receipt of goods sold at Cafe Cinque.) Staff are advised to bring their own until further notice.

**Note to staff** It has been brought to my attention that some staff members are wiping themselves with pages torn from the Policies and Procedures manual. Please be aware that 'purposeful damage to property of Cafe Cinque is a criminal offense and will be dealt with accordingly.' (Chapter 18, section 5)

Since my mother's visit, my sister is determined to prove everyone wrong and make a life for herself in my apartment. She has decided that Coburg is the new Fitzroy and that she could live quite happily here. I came home this evening to find that my Joy Division poster had been replaced by a framed Monet print, and my books had been rearranged to make room for her vintage teacup collection. There were Laura Ashley towels and little soaps in the bathroom, a floral couch in the lounge room, and inspirational magnets on the fridge. A note on our new shabby chic coffee table said that if she was paying 100% of the rent she would furnish the flat the way she saw fit, and that she wanted her name on the lease.

I went into her room, which had been painted mauve, and masturbated on her one thousand-thread Egyptian cotton sheets. I fell asleep, pants down, and waited for her to find me.

You
disgust
me.

After my sister moved out I decided not to advertise for another flatmate. Instead I packed up my belongings, stored them at my mother's, sublet my apartment to some Arts students, and quietly moved into the cafe.

On Friday night I pretended I had important paperwork to attend to and sat in the office while I waited for everyone to leave. By 9pm everyone had gone except the dish pig, who went about his evening routine as though I wasn't there. He shaved and bathed in the kitchen sink, using toiletries stacked on a shelf next to the bleach. He changed into clothes that had been neatly folded and stacked in the storeroom between discarded crockery and old menus. He moisturised with Crabtree and Evelyn rose-scented hand cream, obviously stolen from lost property, paying particular attention to his hands, before putting on a pair of my white cloth gloves. Then he retrieved a pillow, a sheet and a doona from the dry goods cupboard and set them up along the bench seats in High Priority. Apparently he moved in over a month ago, after threatening his landlord during a routine inspection. Somehow he still manages to be late every morning.

I always figured the dish pig spent his evenings plotting my slow and painful death, and was surprised when he pulled out an old copy of *Macbeth*. He read and made notes. For years he has wanted his own theatre company, but he can never afford even the amateur rights to the plays he would like to perform, and over the years he has garnered a reputation as a violent and unpredictable director.

I counted the float for the fifth time and pretended not to notice that the cafe had been transformed into someone's bedroom. He read aloud, as though he was trying to get his head around the words, or perhaps imagining himself on stage, performing the role.

"Are you putting on a play?"

"No, I just like the language."

Eventually he fell asleep, and I unfolded my sleeping bag in Low Priority, as far away from him as possible. I noticed chewing gum under most of the tables.

The next morning I woke up to find the dish pig saluting the sun on the terrazzo. He sets his alarm so he has enough time to pack up before anyone else arrives. I splashed cold water on my face and got changed in the store room. I hid my sleeping bag under the counter and made us both a coffee.

We are not friends, but the dish pig and I have an unspoken agreement to keep our living arrangements a secret and not to get in each other's way. I desperately want to sleep in High Priority but am too afraid to pull rank. This area is fairly quiet at night; the only sounds after 10pm are the trams and a few late-night stragglers from the bar next door. A homeless man takes the croissants from our bread delivery each morning and if I'm awake I have a cigarette with him on the terrazzo. We prepare our own dinner; I survive on leftover focaccias and the occasional muffin, but the dish pig concocts three-course meals from whatever he can find in the kitchen. He sets a table, pours himself a glass of wine and reads the paper. The cleaners sweep and mop around us.

It is almost civil but I sleep in fear every night.

This afternoon I went into the office to steal stationery supplies and found the manager hunched over the desk, crying. The owner has agreed to leave his wife under the proviso that he can continue seeing the girl from the laundromat on a weekly basis. I told her to leave him and assured her that she can do better, but we both know this isn't true.

The cafe has started to look more like a home, and the dish pig and I have settled into a routine. We take turns washing our clothes in the industrial mixer, and the dish pig has fashioned a clothesline from butcher's string, tied from one end of the kitchen to the other. We've planted chilli, tomatoes and silver beet on the terrazzo, in giant vegetable oil tins from the kitchen. We stole soil from the park and fertilised it with used coffee grinds, eggshells and tea leaves.

Now, instead of a sleeping bag on the floor I have a yoga mat from lost property stretched over milk crates. It's comfortable provided I don't move around too much. Our phone chargers are plugged into the wall by the juicer. I use a box of Cock n' Bull Shiraz for a bedside table. The dish pig uses a box of take away coffee cups, on which he has placed the ornamental lamp from next to the register, a few books and a recycled San Pellegrino bottle, which serves as a vase. He steals roses from the park, and each night he smells them before drifting off to sleep. We don't want to draw attention to ourselves using a lot of electricity, so during a rare heatwave we slept on the terrazzo. I was woken up when the young boy from the newsagency accidentally threw a rolled up newspaper at my head.

I went to my mother's house when she was out and retrieved a box labelled 'classic texts' from the garage. I stacked the books neatly behind bags of coffee beans on a shelf above the Gaggia. If I'm having trouble sleeping I run my hands along their spines.

Each night we experiment with mood lighting. With shades made from cut out newspaper and candles found in the storeroom, we can forget that we are squatting in a second rate dining establishment between a bar and a convenience store.

After work tonight I took the tram to Melbourne City Baths for a shower.

When I got back to the café the dish pig was reading *Richard III*. I brushed my teeth and set the alarm on my phone. As I crawled under my doona I whispered, "Now is the winter of our discount rent."

But he was already asleep.


Even though he sleeps with a knife under his pillow, the dish pig is easily the most laid-back person I have ever lived with. He doesn't listen to loud music, he cleans up after himself, and he doesn't speak to me unless it is absolutely necessary.

Last night, however, he made an exception.

"My brother and I had to wash the dishes every night after dinner when we were growing up."

I pretended to be asleep.

"When I was ten, I begged my mother to let me watch the Oscars instead. I told her I had to watch it for school. But I just wanted a night off. She made my brother wash the dishes by himself while I sat in front of the TV with my schoolbooks, pretending to take notes. The ceremony was kind of boring, until Al Pacino won best actor for *Scent of a Woman*. Something clicked in me during his speech. I can still remember exactly how I felt. He talked about encouraging kids from the South Bronx, which hit a nerve, even though I lived in Frankston. During the commercial break, I changed into my dad's wedding suit. I wanted to look like Al Pacino. Most people will tell you they got the acting bug watching a performance, or performing themselves. I got it watching Al Pacino thanking the Academy. It's his fault I wash dishes for a living now. Goodnight."

I stayed awake for a while, wondering if the dish pig met Al Pacino now, would he thank him or try to kill him?

It turns out that fire-proof pyjamas (Christmas, 2010) will catch fire if you put them in the oven to dry. The dish pig was tending the veggie patch and I was googling literary agents on the office computer when the smoke alarm went off. Before we could de-activate it, the fire brigade had arrived. We hid in the garbage disposal area as they flooded the kitchen and then we spent the rest of the night mopping the cafe floor with old tea towels.

Until the replacement oven arrives, our menu is limited, but I have put a positive spin on this and had three thousand flyers printed at Kinko's, inviting local gourmands to support the Raw Food Movement with the Annual Cafe Cinque Naked Lunch. Ethically sourced produce will be served raw and without condiments or flavour enhancers. A three-course meal will be followed by a forty five-minute presentation on Cafe Cinque's recent efforts to protect the environment. This presentation will take place in the dark to save on electricity.

**Policies and Procedures, chapter 16, section 2 – Stock Control**

As this is a busy establishment, it is easy to lose track of inventory and sometimes staff must improvise until stock is replenished. Only necessary items such as milk, coffee, disposable cups and Panadeine Forte may be purchased from local suppliers such as 7Eleven. All other items must be ordered through our regular suppliers. For a full list of necessary items and preferred suppliers, please refer to the Paul Whelan Purchasing Manifest™ on page 611 of this manual.

# Wake in Fright

I woke up last night to find the dish pig holding a rolling pin over my head.

"You're snoring."

"Sorry."

He went back to his bench and fell asleep almost immediately. To avoid further confrontation, I helped myself to the manager's secret stash of Xanax, which I finely chop and sprinkle into the dish pig's wine every night. Now I sleep with a group handle under my pillow just in case.

# Ducks

Despite our living arrangements, the dish pig remains an enigma to me and I am overcome with the urge to know more about him. During his lunch break I followed him to the park across the road, where he feeds the ducks. He threw a mixture of oats, bread crumbs and sultanas into the man-made lake, and spoke to them in funny accents. He has even given some of the ducks names; Michael, Sonny, Lefty and Tony Montana. I hid behind a tree and listened as he told them about his day, his next audition, his favourite film. When a young girl arrived with her mother he offered her some breadcrumbs and told her what kind of ducks they were and where they originate from. He smiled as he walked back to the cafe and I almost liked him.

For the first time since we started living together, the dish pig asked me if I would like to join him for dinner.

"That would be lovely. What are you cooking?"

"Duck."

I moved out the next day.

I am living with my mother until I can afford to move back into my own apartment. My old bedroom is now a scrapbooking den, so on Wednesdays I have to wait until my mother's scrapbooking club have left before I can go to sleep. In an effort to show she cares, my mother wakes me up stupid early in the mornings and offers to make me breakfast.

"Do you want me to make you an omelette?"

"No, thank you."

"Because if you do, you'll have to go and get some eggs. And some milk."

# Hat

The manager wants a hat. She has decided this is the only way to avoid bankruptcy. She worked at a two-hat restaurant a long time ago, before she gave up dancing. Before she started drinking. She told me that the tips are better at hatted restaurants.

The manager knows someone who knows someone who is a food critic for *the Age*. For a small fee, he can arrange for this someone to meet him at Cafe Cinque for lunch next week. Critics do not accept invitations to review restaurants; they prefer the element of surprise. But if the food is amazing, perhaps this critic will be compelled to write about it. It is a huge risk but we have nothing to lose.

It is obvious that Pappadum's food will not inspire a review. The manager works out how much we can afford to spend on an amazing meal, and prays for a last minute cancellation at Vue de Monde. I don't ask her where the money came from, I assume she knows all of the owner's hiding places. Her prayers are answered and we agree that all that effort she put into *Agnes of God* was not a waste after all.

At six o'clock we stand in the lobby of the Rialto Hotel. We are greeted by two staff members with headsets, who direct our attention to a TV screen on the wall offering a view of the kitchen. Then they escort us to the elevator which takes us to the 55th floor, where we are greeted by more people with headsets.

We are grossly out of place in such a high-end establishment but pretend not to notice. The waiter is on to us, especially when I tell him we will require doggy bags for all eight courses. We have the worst table in the restaurant, closest to the toilets. I consider complaining, but remember that this restaurant Googles its guests. If they had time this afternoon, they would have found my blog posts about homogenised milk, a few comments on the Latte Addicts Facebook page, and a news item about the manager's unfortunate shoplifting incident, which she maintains was a misunderstanding.

A young man with an indistinguishable accent introduces himself as our sommelier. Our budget doesn't extend to wine, and he takes it personally when I tell him we will be sticking to water. There are several hushed conversations near the kitchen, and eventually we are given a water jug. I pocket one of the gold-plated teaspoons from the table.

This is the first time the manager and I have socialised outside of the cafe, and the conversation is awkward. We're used to yelling at each other while rushing between the coffee machine and the register, the office and the kitchen. In this way, over several years I have learnt pretty much all there is to know about her. The rest I have gathered from going through her personal belongings in the office. Our table is so big that we can't really hear each other anyway, and the other customers aren't speaking, they just "ooh" and "aah" whenever food is placed in front of them. We decide to concentrate on the reason we are here. I have a notepad so I can write down everything the waiter says about the food. The manager has a camera in case we get the dishes mixed up.

A huge mirror mounted on one wall reflects the open kitchen, so diners can see their food being prepared. Sixteen hands touch my miniscule entree before it comes out.

"State-of-the-art wallaby sliders," announces the waiter.

"Wallaby?"

"It's a small kangaroo, in a bun." he replies, before swanning off to the kitchen.

Native fauna is followed by celeriac, sunflower seed and truffle marshmallow. We share one serve, which amounts to half a mouthful each, and put the other aside to take home. I notice that the manager's gold plated teaspoon has also disappeared.

At the next table, a young woman flirts shamelessly with the waiter, oblivious to the fact that her boyfriend is about to propose. He has the ring in his left hand, and fingers it nervously.

The second course is a complicated affair involving a beaker and a Bunsen burner. I scrutinise the waiter's face for signs of a prank, I search the walls for hidden cameras. The manager inhales her serve, and, deciding it is too much effort to set up a science experiment in the cafe, I do the same.

The sommelier eyeballs us each time he passes with a bottle of wine.

The waiters circle the tables at a relaxed pace, like goldfish. They avoid bumping into each other, as if their course is pre-determined. Even when it appears that they will collide, one switches direction at the last minute, to collect a dirty plate or refill a wine glass. At Cafe Cinque, we are only like goldfish in that we begin each shift having forgotten that we did the same thing the previous day and the day before that, because that is the only way to get through it. But some things are built into our memories. Certain chores, when done often enough, become second nature. Like using your right hip to open the swinging door that leads to the kitchen, swivelling to fit between tables 4 and 5, or dropping your head to avoid hitting the hanging plant by the window.

As it grows dark outside we are served pigeon with Jerusalem artichoke, porcini mushrooms and smoked hay.

"I'm not sure they have hay in India, let alone wallabies."

The manager takes a photo before eating. "Tastes like chicken."

I pretend to admire the view.

The young couple receive their dessert before us and we wait for her to notice the ring on top of her violet-and-rosemary-infused pannacotta. She squeals and the waiter is forgotten. Champagne is brought to the table. We are offered a glass and I make sure it is free before accepting it. She takes photos of the ring in her dessert with her iPhone and calls her mother. Suddenly lonely, I wonder what Flat White is doing. I ask the waiter to bring me a Scotch.

The manager and I sit in silence, depressed in the knowledge that we will never be proposed to in a fancy restaurant.

Our pannacotta arrives. The manager takes a bite and looks towards the kitchen appreciatively. As I move to take my half, her face changes, then she spits the dessert back onto her plate.

"BASTARD!"

I recognise him from the dartboard she made of his photo last

Valentine's day; THE ONE, arranging wallaby sliders on an oversized plate. Within seconds she is in the kitchen, brandishing a cast iron pot. The other chefs are huddled in a corner as she stands over THE ONE and delivers a scathing review of his character and his cooking ability, rehearsed and perfected over many years.

At first THE ONE doesn't recognise her; she hasn't aged well. But when he does, he grabs the largest knife he can find before ducking under the bench and screaming, "Please don't hurt me; I have children!"

"WITH THE KITCHEN HAND?!"

He doesn't answer, which I guess means yes, with the kitchen hand.

The waiters rush to gather our belongings and it takes five people in headsets to restrain the manager. When she finally calms down and hands over the cast iron pot, we are escorted to the elevator. "We're not leaving without our doggy bags," I tell them. They give us our individually wrapped leftovers and tell us never to return. No one mentions the bill.

Outside, the manager suggests a nightcap, and I remind her that she has been banned from most places in the CBD, and that the only bar which will let her in is Cherry.

"Please Paul, I need a fucking drink. And maybe something to eat."

We grab a couple of sausage rolls from a 7Eleven and make our way down Flinders Lane. At Cherry we are the oldest people by at least a decade, but it's dark so it doesn't matter. Skinny boys in skinny jeans thrash about on the tiny stage. Most people stand by the bar and nod their heads in time to the music, but one enthusiastic young woman does an entire routine up the front. She twirls and skips and jumps and we wait for her to get dizzy and fall down, but she has energy to burn. She doesn't appear embarrassed. She seems happy to pass the time dancing alone. I have never been capable of such joy.

When the band stops, I find the manager talking to a bar stool. I tell her I'm tired, hand her the doggy bags and take a tram to Flat White's apartment, where I spend the rest of the evening sitting on his door step, working up the courage to knock on his door. At 6am I get up and walk to work.

# Critic

The critic arrived earlier than expected, so I kicked some people out of high priority and seated her by the window.

She asked for a *caffe latte* in an Italian accent, but I let her stay. Then she asked for a menu but I explained that we do degustation after 11am, and assured her that she would enjoy the food. All other orders were put on hold, and I ran to the kitchen to supervise. Pappadum assured me that there are no wallabies, bottle brush, marshmallows or Jerusalem artichokes in India, so we put mango pickles on the side of everything. Pappadum's mother sent him a huge batch when he told her of his promotion.

"State-of-the-art wallaby slider," I announced, solemnly. I placed it in the middle of the table. She looked confused.

"It's a small kangaroo, in a focaccia," I told her, before swanning off to the kitchen. I watched from behind the swing door as she pushed the plate to one side. She took no notes.

The truffle marshmallow had not fared well in the freezer, so I spread it on naan bread and presented it as a South Indian special-ty. I had to remove the half-finished coffees to make room for the oversized plate. The critic told me she lived in India for many years and that she never saw a truffle there. I told her that her last review contained two superlatives, three grammatical errors and one misuse of the word 'fusion.'

The morning went downhill from there. She asked the new girl to bring her a menu and ordered some slow-boiled eggs, which she returned, complaining that the yolk was discoloured. The new girl referred the issue to me.

"What colour was it?"

"Green."

"Green-green or yellow-green?"

"Post-apocalyptic green."

I told the new girl that if she resolved the issue with minimum fuss, I would consider shortening her probationary period. She jotted a few things down on her notepad and galloped over to table 8. She apologised to the critic and explained that "the chicken who laid this particular egg did not have enough water this morning, which is the risk you take when eating organic free range. While we understand if you do not want to eat the egg, we want to assure you that there is nothing wrong with it; it is merely an egg from a dehydrated chicken, and while you can lead a horse to water, you can't force free range chickens to drink."

The critic left, and later we received an email from her explaining why Cafe Cinque is not eligible for a hat. She offered a few suggestions for improvement ("know your market, train your wait staff") and wished us the best of luck. She also suggested that when a customer asks for directions to the ladies' room, we do not give them half a roll of toilet paper from behind the counter. An article appeared on her blog about Melbourne's most random dining experiences. We made the top five. We also received several phone calls from animal liberation groups asking us to change poultry suppliers and a visit from the health inspector.

I wrote my own review on Urbanspoon;

> Fusion degustation at Cafe Cinque cafe/Indian restaurant/bar
> Not since Vue de Monde have I eaten such a dazzling concoction of gourmet fare. Why hasn't this establishment got a hat? Two thumbs up.

To which my mother replied:

> Paul, have you stopped taking your medication? Call me.

# Writers' festival

In an attempt to draw a more literary crowd during the Writers' Festival, I gave the new girl the task of naming menu items after famous books. After checking supplies in the kitchen she could only think of one: *Green Eggs and Spam*.

> **Policies and Procedure chapter 13, section 8 – Irrational customers**
>
> Irrational customers are not to be mistaken for difficult or demanding customers, although they can be both difficult and demanding. Irrational customers will blow small incidents out of proportion and turn insignificant mistakes into major issues. They will try and trick you into seeing the world through their eyes, with questions like "How would you feel if someone gave you the wrong sandwich?" Do not answer these questions. Simply say "You are being irrational and I would like you to leave," or "You are being irrational and I am going to refer you to my manager/personal mentor/the police."

This morning I asked the manager to sign a waiver.
"What's this for?"
"My novel."
"Is it about me?"
"No, it's about me. But you make an appearance."
"I thought you had been rejected by every publisher in Australia."
"I am considering self-publishing."
"All the legal documents in the world won't save you if you mention the Tequila Incident."
"Of course not."
What she doesn't realise is that the Tequila Incident has been heavily documented on Urbanspoon. After another fight with the owner and a bottle of Mexico's finest, she passed out next to the kitchen door and wet herself. No one wanted to touch her so we left her propped up against the wall and put a tablecloth over her head.

Fortunately it was during the Fringe Festival so most people assumed she was an art installation.

The owner turned up during the lunch rush and tried to remove the Gaggia. I threw myself on top of it and yelled "You will not take this machine!" When he tried to pry me off I rapped him on the knuckles with a group handle. He took the grinder instead, which isn't technically ours. We lease it from our coffee suppliers, but I can't ask for a replacement because we owe them thousands of dollars. Now I have to get our beans ground at Latte Cino up the street. The staff there are very understanding; their boss arrived during a weekend lunch rush and took all the light fittings.

> **Note to customers** Due to reasons we cannot disclose, we are no longer serving food.

I arrived to work this morning to find a giant padlock on the front door. At first I thought that the dish pig had finally declared war on the world and was hiding under table 4, waiting for me to break in so he could attack me with a weapon made from items in the lost property basket. But then I noticed him curled up in the corner of the terrazzo; he had been evicted by the sheriff last night. His belongings were in milk crates, stacked behind the gas heaters.

"I suppose you blame me for this."

He didn't reply, he just lit another cigarette and watched me as I stood in front of the door, unsure of what to do for the next eight hours.

Eventually I managed to crawl through the window overlooking the garbage disposal area. The furniture, the appliances and my Gaggia had been removed, but the Policies and Procedures manuals were still in the storeroom. I spent the rest of the day sitting in an empty office weighing up my options.

# Sabbatical

Cafe Cinque has been closed for several weeks. The owner of the cafe resides in Barwon Prison until he can post bail. The manager has set up camp outside the prison to make sure there are no female visitors from the laundromat. After a short trip to Healesville with money I found under the floorboards in the office, I moved back into my flat and offered to re-open Cafe Cinque under the following conditions:

- I will return under the title of Executive Barista, and may hire an Assistant to the Executive Barista to help with all administrative duties.
- I will be paid more.
- All profits will go towards posting bail, but any cash found under office floorboards or behind the staff toilet may be used for Executive Barista's foreign travel and/or liquor supply.

Then I posted a notice on the Café Cinque Facebook page, stating that the café would re-open soon under new management.

---

**Urbanspoon** Congratulations to the newly appointed Executive Barista! I hope you asked for a pay rise so you can finally start paying back that money you owe me. GourmetDi.

---

# COFFEE CHAIN

# Hostile Takeover

In order to post bail, my boss has sold Cafe Cinque to a well-known coffee chain, which offered to re-hire existing full time staff. While the cafe is being refurbished with funky light fittings and beige couches, we have been forced to attend Staff Training, a series of 'fun' team building exercises and informative lectures about the way in which this amazing organisation is 'inspiring and nurturing the human spirit, one cup at a time.' During these sessions we are referred to as 'partners' in the company, but have been informed that we will still be treated like regular employees. I have also been told that my Policies and Procedures Manual is no longer required, and that my beloved Gaggia will be replaced by a bigger, better machine. I must wear a green apron and be nice to the customers. I must make flavoured beverages in oversized take away cups. I must listen to Norah Jones. I have decided not to quit until I am up to date on the rent.

# Rude Shock

As my new employers prefer to serve their oversized flavoured beverages in reusable recyclable 100% biodegradable paper cups, there is no need for a dish washer. The dish pig, never one to miss an opportunity to make my life hell, has answered their call for 'adaptable self-motivated, passionate, creative team players' and after undergoing their Accelerated Staff Management Program, will be my new boss. During a break from our team building exercises this morning, he quietly informed me of his plans to make my life fucking miserable, *one cup at a time.*

My manager lasted exactly twenty minutes into our first day of trading. She didn't qualify for the Accelerated Staff Management Program, so was forced to accept a customer service position. We stood in the ladies' toilet and examined our reflections in the mirror; two adults in full-length aprons, name badges and baseball caps.

"Fuck this. I'm going back to Schnitz n' Tits."

"Don't you think you're a little old to be serving chicken parma without a bra?"

"I'd rather go topless than wear a name badge. It's about dignity, Paul."

She didn't bother to quit, she just walked out, and I haven't seen her since.

# New Order

On his first day as Store Manager, the dish pig hired a new barista. Spiro is the current National Champion Barista, a fitness fanatic and an all-round top bloke. He can do twenty two push ups in the twenty two seconds it takes to pour the perfect shot. I hate him. I have been relegated to the register, where I must greet each customer with; "Welcome to your local coffee shop! We hope your visit is an enjoyable one. What would you like to drink today?" Customers rarely know what they would like, as the drinks menu is so confusing. There is no such thing as a regular coffee, if someone orders one I must ask a series of questions to work out exactly what it is they want. "Regular size or regular milk? Or your regular coffee which you have been drinking for several years? By regular do you mean drip, or espresso-based? And if you mean drip, which drip? We have three on offer today..."

According to the new training manual, after establishing which coffee the customer would like, the person at the register must 'repeat and confirm' the order by yelling it back at the customer, yelling it out to the barista, who must repeat it to himself, then announce it to the world when the beverage is made. While this is humiliating, it is nice to be able to yell over Norah Jones.

"Grande triple skinny hazelnut latte, no froth, low-fat whip!"

"Venti soy mocha Frappuccino, no whip!"

"Ethically sourced single-origin Guatemalan medium roast drip, whip on the side!"

Sometimes the drinks get lost in translation and the customer becomes irate. Sometimes I will purposefully mess up the order then blame Spiro. The dish pig notes it all down in his big black book and it is only a matter of time before I am out on the street, hassling passers-by to sample miniature versions of our signature iced coffee.

Having passed a day-long exam, Spiro has earned the title Coffee Master, and is permitted to wear a black apron. He believes he is beyond constructive criticism and did not appreciate me pointing out that the vanilla macchiato he made at 8.01am was over-extracted. I have been timing his shots from behind the pastry case.

Getting rid of him will be difficult, because he is a hit with the female customers. When he's steaming their milk, and they ask for it to be extra hot, he replies "How hot? Hotter than you?" They pass their phone numbers over the counter. He keeps a log of all the ones he has slept with on the side of the machine.

## Staff Meetings

occur weekly and resemble group therapy sessions. They are led by the company's in-house psychotherapist. No important decisions are made at store level; instead, we are encouraged to discuss our feelings. How did we feel when we made a coffee? How did we feel when a customer said thank you? How did we feel when a customer didn't say thank you? At first we were reluctant to be so candid, but now we compete to reveal the most about ourselves. Each meeting ends with a motivational quote, no doubt found on the internet. This week's was *"Men's best successes come after their disappointments."*

## Asset protection

I am careful to show only my good side to the many security cameras mounted behind the register and above the front door. This means that when customers place an order they must address the side of my head. When head office queried the till being out while I was on shift, I explained that if I looked down at the register I would be caught on camera with a double chin, and demanded a Braille key pad.

## Traffic control

I have been removed from the register and given a radio head set. During the morning rush I have to approach each person waiting in line and ask for their order before they reach the counter, then repeat it into my little microphone. As I am the only one with a headset, this order doesn't actually go anywhere, and the customers have to repeat their request when they finally get to the register. Apparently people are more likely to wait in a line once they have placed an order. After the rush I am permitted behind the counter to assist with iced beverages, but under no circumstance am I allowed to touch the blenders.

During this evening's staff meeting, everyone agreed that a customer service representative has no right to pass judgement on the Coffee Master, and that I should go through the proper channels to address any issues I may have with Spiro's performance. The in-house therapist placed a hand on my shoulder and asked, "Paul, do you trust Spiro to do his job properly?"

"Yes. Yes, I do."

"We are going to do a little exercise aimed at developing trust between partners."

He asked me to stand, and asked Spiro to stand a short distance behind me. I had to fold my arms across my chest and slowly fall backwards and say, "I trust you." Spiro promised to catch me before I hit the ground. He caught me at the last second, but then dropped me on the floor to punch the air with his fists and exclaim, "Yes! I rock!"

Then the dish pig offered to do the same exercise with me. I fell back and he didn't catch me. He said I had to learn not to trust everyone; that sometimes people steal or try to short change us or are dishonest and that I should harden up.

Dan from Ginger Lee has found me on Facebook and wants to be friends, but he is already friends with my mother, which means I would have to change my privacy settings so that friends of friends cannot read my wall, likes and dislikes and use Facebook to spy on me. *Ignore.*

# Writing class

Everyone has changed their book to be about vampires, and all are aimed at the YA market. Except Birkie of course. I don't actually know anything about vampires. I've never met one, unless you count Stryker Stormbringer, who did a trial at Café Cinque three years ago. He had his name changed by deed poll from Nigel and his front teeth had been filed to points. I sent him home when he refused to remove his cape, which was in violation of OH and S Policy 114. When he asked why he didn't get the job I told him "Because you suck," but vampires don't have a sense of humour. He only wanted evening work anyway.


The dish pig is away for a week completing his Advanced Leadership Training. The office wall is covered with certificates he has earned by attending all the workshops available to him as an adaptable self-motivated, passionate, creative team player; Accelerated Human Resources and Partner Engagement, Advanced Product Knowledge and Customer Engagement, Accelerated Product Penetration and Customer Retention. I have never doubted his talent as an actor, but I am thoroughly impressed by his ability to fool an entire organisation into believing he is the ultimate employee. He is the first to arrive and the last to leave, and has energy to burn. He punches the air, he punches his own fist, he shakes your hand when you get to work, comes behind the counter just to pat you on the back and say disconcerting things like, "I really appreciate what you're doing for us here, Paul." At the beginning of each shift he makes us hold hands in a circle and says "Let's hit a home run today, guys." He even interacts with the customers; moving from table to overstuffed chair asking people if they are having a good day. He has everyone fooled except me. Before he left he pat me on the back so hard I fell and hit my head on the top of the display cabinet.

The district manager is watching the store for a week. He has been with the company for seven years, "The seven most challenging and fulfilling years of my life." He believes there is a lesson for everyone in everything we do. When I approached him about a pay rise he said, "The fact that you are doing your part to enrich other people's lives should be reward enough." He also punches the air and pats partners on the back, but he is not acting. If he's in the store during our early morning hand holding ritual, he asks God to give us the strength to serve our community with grace and humility. This morning I caught him saying grace before eating a double choc chip muffin.

# Reunion

On my way home, I stopped to buy bottled water and recognised it immediately: my Gaggia, stuck in a third-rate establishment on Swanston professing to sell "coffee and cappuccinos." I ordered a short black and asked the barista how he scored such a beautiful machine.

"Ours broke and the coffee supplier gave us this piece of shit. I wanted one with a neon light."

I threw my coffee on the counter, yelled "Animal!" and stormed out.

# First Impressions

My Policies and Procedures manual has been replaced with a twelve hundred-page document titled *Journey of Discovery*. Partners have been issued with small green passports, in which we are to record our impressions of various coffee blends. During a tasting, we take turns offering adjectives previously used to describe customers; *fruity, nutty, dirty, acidic.* We are encouraged to think of food or situations that complement certain blends. The new girl suggests that the house blend is 'a bright, citrusy explosion of spicy nectar best enjoyed sitting on a tram reading *Frankie* magazine munching on a toffee apple," and is given a free plunger. She is considered a High Performing Partner and has been issued with a team leader badge. She spends hours deciding where each partner should stand and what they should do to ensure maximum productivity. She instructed me to divide my time between the product shelf, where I am to dust packets of Special Blend, and the pastry cabinet, where I am to rotate the savoury scones.

If I want to be a barista again I have to study the Beverage Resource Manual. I am not allowed to take it home, in case it is stolen by the competition, so I read it during my lunch break. I am not even permitted to make myself a coffee during my break. I have to stand in line like everyone else, 'to get the full customer experience.' I refuse to queue for a Spiro-made coffee, so have resorted to snorting ground coffee to get me through the day.

**Inquiry Att:** Communications Officer

**From:** Paul Whelan Partner Number 3251713

**RE:** Drinks menu

While studying the beverage resource manual in my quest for self-improvement, I noticed that the drinks menu is a curious combination of Italian and made-up words.

Was this company inspired by Anthony Burgess and his clever use of English and Russian to create street slang in A Clockwork Orange?

**To:** Partner No. 3251713

**RE:** Drinks Menu

It is part of our mission to create a new way of enjoying coffee and a new language to describe the act of enjoying coffee. The words which you refer to as 'made-up' are, in fact, trademarks of our company and are not to be used outside the store unless for approved promotional activity. Who is Anthony Burgess?

Back from leadership training, the dish pig asked to see me in his office to discuss my Individual Development and Proposed Career Trajectory. I asked the new girl to come with me. I know he wouldn't hesitate to use extreme violence in front of others, but I figured I could use the new girl as a buffer if he tried anything. I stood behind her as he congratulated me on being accepted into the Accelerated Barista Certification training program. Despite the protestors who have been camped out on the footpath since we opened, we are busy, and the powers that be have agreed to a second person on the machine.

Even though this position means being stuck in a corner with nowhere to run if the dish pig came at me with a large plunger, I accepted, thinking I could always use Spiro as a buffer. I thanked him and went back to work.

It's difficult to zone out here and just go through the motions until closing time. Norah Jones and fusion jazz are frequently interrupted by pre-recorded in-store announcements: "We are thankful for our partners," "Productivity is up three percent," and "Have you tried our new pumpkin cinnamon-flavoured hot chocolate with low-fat caramel whip?"

It was bound to happen eventually: someone I went to high school with came into the cafe today. She spotted me hiding behind the pastry cabinet, suddenly fascinated by the savoury scones.

"Look at you in your green apron!"

I pretended she had mistaken me for somebody else and prodded the scones with a pair of tongs.

"What are you doing here, Paul?"

"Research."

I avoided further explanation by crawling under the pastry cabinet and staying there until she left.

## Just say yes

My employers have implemented a new policy so that we are known as the can-do cafe, where any reasonable request may be satisfied and nothing is too much trouble. Can I re- charge my phone using your power point? Yes. Can I have a grande cappuccino for the price of a regular drip? Yes. Can you put a dash of whiskey from my hip flask into my soy chai? Yes. Do you accept foreign currency? Yes. Do we accept personal cheques? Yes. Do we mind people's children while they go shopping? Yes. Would the cafe act as guarantor on a bank loan? Yes. Would we mind this suitcase until the owner picks it up the next day? Yes. Yes. Yes. Yes.

# No

Did you put alcohol in someone's drink? No. Did you accept a personal check for two hundred dollars? Not exactly. Did you keep this bag full of drugs in the office overnight? Sort of. Did you lock three children under the age of five in the staff toilet for an entire afternoon? Maybe. Do you know that we are in a lot of shit? Yes.

I spent the afternoon at head office where I was lectured for three hours on the meaning of *reasonable* request. The woman with the whiskey was a plant, but the children and drug dealer were real so the police are involved.

As I was simply following company policy, they could not charge me or fire me, but they have decided to re-write their policies with the view that some partners are not able to think for themselves. Three media liaison officers were working on a strategy to combat the publicity my actions may attract. On my way home I called all three newspapers offering to tell my side of the story for a small fee.

# Celebrity

As I can no longer be trusted to take orders, I have been moved to the condiment bar, where I am to assist customers with lids, stirrers, chocolate sprinkles, cinnamon and nutmeg. A camera man from *A Current Affair* arrived to film me re stocking the sugar sticks, but I was upstaged by the new girl, studying a diagram which outlined the correct way to wipe the bench with a wet cloth.

# Promotion

After three weeks of intense study and a day-long exam, I am finally allowed behind the coffee machine, on the proviso that I do not interact with the customers. Only Spiro can be trusted with the more complicated task of steaming milk, so I must stand next to him for eight hours a day and pull shots. He is furious that he has to share the machine. "Why can't we just send him to another store?"

"Why should I go to another store? I was here first."

He also complained about my barista's holster. "You look like you're going to war."

"I look like I take my job seriously."

Later, I received a letter from head office asking me not to wear it, as it is not part of the uniform.

When it's busy, one person is responsible for making sure the coffees go out in order. Naturally, this person should be me, as the dockets come to my side of the machine. But Spiro has other ideas.

"You don't call the shots, you pull the shots. When I say so. You are here to assist me. I'm the Coffee Master."

"I was making espresso when you were wearing nappies."

"That's because you're old."

I know he likes to pour the milk as soon as the shot is ready, so I like to remove the shots at the last second and throw them away.

"I didn't like the crema on that one. I'll have to do it again."

He stands there, furious, swirling the milk in the jug so it doesn't settle, keeping an eye on the thermometer.

"Sorry, Spiro. Some of us have standards."

Of course, now that I am on the machine I can drink coffee anytime I want; it's my job to make sure the shots are not over-extracted and bitter. But I prefer to snort it. I collect small amounts in my apron pocket and sneak off to the toilet at regular intervals throughout the day.

It's company policy to leave the manager's phone number next to the counter with a sign that reads "How are we doing?" I make sure I call it every night around 11 to tell him.

"Hello?"

"I think we're doing okay."

"You have a death wish."


Spiro has filed a complaint about the fact that I bring my own apron to work. I bought a black one from Cedar Hospitality with his share of the tips.

"Whoa, whoa, whoa, whoa, whoa! What the fuck?! You can't just wear a black apron. You have to earn it."

"It's not like Kung Fu."

"It's *exactly* like Kung Fu. My moves are the result of hours and hours of practice."

"The green apron shows up the dirt."

"Then take it home and wash it."

My apron was confiscated and after lunch the district manager sat me down and explained the importance of having goals and working to achieve those goals.

"We know that you are capable of applying yourself, Paul. You worked hard to become a barista. But by wearing a black apron, you are being deceitful. We don't want customers to think their shots are being prepared by someone more qualified than you are."

He made me sign three documents that said I understood our conversation before I returned to the machine.

Then Spiro accused me of hiding the steam wand nozzle from his side of the machine. I may have misplaced it while I was cleaning. I may have tried to remove the entire steam wand, but this required too many tools and an intimate knowledge of this particular machine. He eventually found it soaking in a cup of water and espresso cleaner behind 60kgs of Christmas Blend. I told him I put it here so it wouldn't get lost. Because it took him so long to find it, we were unable to serve white coffees for the rest of the day. He took the nozzle home with him at the end of his shift. Technically, this is theft, and I have reported him to Upper Upper Management in the form of an anonymous letter.

Today Spiro accused me of invading his personal space and painted a white line on the floor between us. I reported him for vandalism and we were both sent to head office for counselling, where we were asked to put our concerns in writing. The counsellor used war- time negotiation tactics to help us reconcile our differences. I am not allowed to interrupt Spiro when he lists my short comings and he is not to interrupt me when I complain of his blatant disregard for my coffee making experience. When we realised that we wouldn't be paid overtime for this, we agreed to an Accelerated Bonding Session. At the end of it we each received a certificate commending us for our ability to communicate and work as a team. Then the counsellor gave us a raw egg. "For the next week you must work together to ensure that this egg remains intact."

I dropped it on the way out and made a joke about the three second rule. Spiro did not laugh.

The new girl has been given another promotion and spends half the week in head office. She asked me to look over her new contract. "You're getting paid HOW MUCH to hashtag caramel latte?"

"I'm the Social Media Manager."

She still has to work two full days in the store so she doesn't lose touch with the customers, but she spends most of this time taking photos of people with foam moustaches.

I'm not allowed to have my Moleskine out at work so I keep my coffee passport in my apron pocket and when inspired, I write. I left it in the men's toilet yesterday so when I got to work this morning I was called into the office. The dish pig would do everything in his power to keep me away from the coffee machine, but he would never interfere with my writing, just as I would never do anything to jeopardise his acting. We have an unspoken agreement that creative endeavours are off-limits. The district manager, however, had no qualms about report-ing me to head office for defacing company property. He quoted page 702 of the Learning Journey; "All secondary employment must take second priority to all existing job requirements." I considered suing them for plagiarism but then I remembered that I had copied some of their policies from the web when I started writing my Policies and Procedures manual.

My passport was confiscated and I was issued with a new one, which I am only allowed to write in during tastings, under strict supervision. I have to return it afterwards. So now I am using reusable, recyclable 100% biodegradable paper bags to take notes, which I fold and hide in my underwear.

It has taken me a week to notice but Spiro has been removing parts of my bike during his lunch break. I assumed I'd lost the bell in traffic, but on Tuesday night I had to ride home without lights, on Wednesday the seat had gone and this evening all that remained was the frame and my helmet. He is holding the rest of the bike ransom until I apologise for hiding the nozzle. I refuse to admit any wrongdoing so I have to take the tram to work.

# The 8

carries an army of baristas from Moreland Rd through the city and past Chapel St. Surrounded by a sea of black, I am reminded that I am not the only person who wakes up before sunrise to slave away behind a counter. I feel a sense of camaraderie with these people but not enough to make eye contact. No one makes eye contact. The tram is quiet. No one speaks. Some rest their heads against the windows; one girl has fallen asleep standing up. What would happen if we all decided to stay home? Could this city survive without coffee for one day?

You can tell where in the city each person works by the way we are dressed. We all wear black but there are subtle differences to our attire; those who work the cafes in Degraves St and the surrounding laneways favour skinny black jeans, piercings, tattoos and vintage trainers. Those working the Paris end towards Spring St wear dress pants, long sleeved shirts and leather shoes. Some wear faded polo shirts with the name of a coffee supplier embroidered on the left breast. These people work for middle-aged Italians who use established suppliers like Vittoria, Coffex and Lavazza. They crowd the busy footpaths of Collins and Bourke with oversized umbrellas and street barriers.

I am always conscious of how I smell when riding public transport; a mixture of coffee and stale milk. The coffee gets into your pores and stays there. I've never taken enough time off work to know if it ever leaves you. My right index finger is stained from years of flicking the handle on the grinder. My right palm is stained from removing excess coffee grinds off the group handles. Nothing gets the smell out of your clothes. I didn't mind so much this morning. We all carried that same stale coffee smell with us as one by one we dragged ourselves off the tram and disappeared into the city.

I moved towards the back door just before my stop and my green apron fell out of my bag. All eyes were on me as I bent down to pick it up and I know what they were all thinking: I am not one of them. I am the enemy. I can no longer call myself a barista. I decided I would have the money for a new bike by the end of the week.

Just before closing I looked up from the machine to find Flat White sitting by the door. Table four no longer existed, so he was seated in an overstuffed chair, newspaper on his lap. I don't think he noticed that the cafe had changed. He sat there as though it was completely natural for him to reappear after so long. I wasn't sure if he had seen me so l pretended to be absorbed in the inner workings of the coffee grinder. I've been carrying a copy of my manuscript with me for months on the off chance that he came back. There is a coffee stain on the cover. I'm not sure he will even remember our last conversation. "Where have you been?" I wanted to say. "It's so nice to see a familiar face. I've missed you!"

Instead I told him, "You can't sit there."

I placed a reserved sign on the chair and went back to the machine, ignoring him until he left, without a coffee.

# Holster

I've considered self-publishing, which is expensive. My barista's wage barely covers my living expenses, but there is potential profit to be made from my barista's holster, which is collecting dust on my bedroom floor. After calculating how many holsters I need to sell to pay for my first print run, I uploaded a photo and a brief description of the Whelan Holster to the IP Australia website. A few days later, I received a call from someone at the patent office, wanting to verify a few details. After a brief discussion, she explained that I can't patent something designed by someone else.

"But I invented a different use for the holster."

"No, you just filled the holster with different things."

I decided to sell it without a patent and placed a full page ad in *Crema* magazine with my district manager's credit card; *The Whelan Holster – for gun baristas.* I included a photo of myself pulling a toothpick out of a side pocket with the slogan *Choose your weapon.* I priced them at $149.95 plus delivery and sold one, to my mother, even after I explained that someone who drinks tea does not require coffee making tools or a holster to put them in. "It's for your Aunty Edna. She can wear it when she's pruning her roses."

# Intervention

The dish pig, the new girl and the in-house therapist cornered me as I was coming out of the store room. "We can't help but notice that your behaviour is more erratic than usual. Is there anything you'd like to tell us?"

"Like what?"

The new girl reached around and removed 30 grams of ground Colombian Roast from my back pocket. "I was going to take it home and put it in a plunger." Then she held me down while the dish pig retrieved parcels of ground coffee from my front pockets, my apron pocket, my sleeve and my socks. They missed the 30 grams I had taped to my leg.

# Community

As partners in this company, we are expected to take an active interest in the world, and interact with members of the local community. Once a month we can recommend a different charitable event to support. The new girl suggested we give leftover muffins and pastries to the homeless at the end of each day. She was told that this is against health and safety regulations as it is almost impossible to warn homeless people that some food may contain traces of nuts. No free plunger.

# Blackmail

It turns out that the 'highly adaptable self-motivated passionate creative team players' that I am now forced to work with are also highly promiscuous. While dutifully placing used, reusable recyclable 100% biodegradable oversized paper cups into the recycling bin out the back, I stumbled upon the District Manager and the new Shift Supervisor engaging in some rather questionable Team Bonding exercises. I pretended not to notice, and moved one of the cameras from the front of the store to the back. All incriminating footage will be used to assist me in my quest to obtain financial compensation for the emotional trauma caused by seeing my Shift Supervisor in nothing but a green apron.

## Management

My foray into low-budget film has earned me a new bike and a promotion. I am now Area Supervisor, a position which comes with many perks, the main one being that I am superior to the manager formerly known as the dish pig. I have a company car, a company credit card and a company phone. I spend my days driving from one chain store to another ensuring that they all look the same. Most of these stores are in the outer suburbs so I have asked for special permission to carry a weapon.

## Anxiety Attack

My new position as Area Supervisor comes with much responsibility. Not only must I ensure that all the stores look exactly the same, I must also check that each staff member displays the appropriate levels of energy and enthusiasm in order to 'connect with, laugh with and uplift the lives of our customers'. While inspecting my sixteenth store in two days, I became disorientated. I checked that the Organic Shade Grown Mexican blend was adequately signposted, forgot which store I was in and had a mild anxiety attack. A trainee barista left her work station and directed me to a beige couch in the far corner of the store, and instructed me to breathe deeply into a reusable, recyclable 100% biodegradable paper bag. As this is a common occurrence amongst staff members forced to spend time in multiple stores, my request for sick leave was granted immediately.

I have decided to use this time off to write. Inspired by Fyodor, who did his best work after his exile to Siberia, I placed the following ad on Gumtree:

## Wanted: Short-term accommodation past the tram line. Must be within cycling distance to Dan Murphy's or equivalent.

I received several responses, but the only one I can afford is a granny flat in Craigieburn, which is not only beyond the tram line but also nowhere near a train station. I've packed 28 bottles of merlot and some sliced bread. My mother has agreed to give me a lift.

"Are you sure you know what you're doing, Paul? This seems an extravagance, especially since you haven't bothered to sublet your own flat."

"I am determined to fix my book. There is nothing else to do out here."

After turning off the highway we got lost. All the streets looked the same, and according to the GPS we were driving through fields.

We arrived at the house just after dark and the owner lead me to a self-contained unit at the back of the yard. My mother insisted on checking that it was clean, and then I stood out the front and waved to her as she passed the house three times before finding the way out and onto the highway.

I opened a bottle of wine and put my toiletries in the bathroom. I placed my Moleskine on the desk, and then moved it to the bed, in case I woke up in the middle of the night with an idea. Then I moved the desk to face the wall. I put the television in the linen cupboard. After rifling through my bag and all of my pockets, I went to the back of the main house and knocked on the door. The woman answered in her bathrobe.

"Yes?"

"Could I borrow a pen?"

She closed the door. I was about to go back to the granny flat when she opened it again and handed me two felt tip pens. The lids had been chewed.

"Thanks."

This morning I was woken by someone from Jim's Mowing attacking the hedges with a chainsaw. It was almost noon, so I went straight to my desk. My memoir could be a tell-all book about everyone who has pissed me off over the years. But I don't remember names. I only remember drinks. For almost ten years my life has revolved around an endless list of coffees, served at the same time, day after day after day. By 4pm all I had was a list of hot beverages. I couldn't even make them rhyme to create a poem.

I decided to go for a walk and clear my head. I left a trail of bread crumbs to help me find my way back. After walking for several hours, I gave up. By this time it was dark so I couldn't see the bread crumbs. I was eventually picked up by the police, as several residents had reported a suspicious looking person in the area. They drove me back to the house, where the woman assured them that I was not dangerous.

I begged my mother to come and get me as I wasn't confident I could find my way off the estate. The owner of the granny flat refused to give me a refund, and my mother felt obliged to remind me that Dostoyevsky didn't have the luxury of being able to leave Siberia whenever he wanted.

I called head office to discuss resigning from my position as Area Manager and returning to the cafe as a barista as soon as possible.

# Peace offering

On my first day back I made a special coffee for the dish pig; three shots of espresso blended with milk and topped with whipped cream, on which I placed two coffee beans for eyes, and some chocolate sprinkles for facial hair. He eyed it suspiciously.

"It's a Frap Pacino."

I could tell he was touched, but I didn't expect him to walk out as a result. I found him out the back burning his apron. "I'm an actor." He didn't bother to quit, he just left. And I haven't seen him since.

On my second day back, a mysterious figure in a dark hoodie approached the counter and handed me a piece of paper with a web address. I assumed it was my mother's new way of getting my attention, but when I typed the address into my phone, I was directed to a site devoted to comments from partners all over the world, complaining about the way they are treated by both their employers and the customers. It is possible to send this company broke by forcing them to spend hundreds of thousands of dollars defending themselves against accusations such as:

"My manager uses emotional blackmail to make me work overtime."

"I was forced to drink coffee against my will in the name of product knowledge, despite my ulcer."

There are also hundreds of references to my appearance on *A Current Affair*. The words 'hero' and 'inspiration' are used a lot. I joined the site as Triple Rosetta. My first post was not a complaint, but a call to action; a picture of two group handles crossed over accompanied by the slogan "Baristas of the world unite!" Within a few hours, my slogan had been shared thousands of times. I left it to someone else to figure out what we were united against. I'm sure that between them Chai Killer, Death Before Decaf and Grande Triple Threat could work it out. Eventually one of them posted a list of demands; most of them unimaginative, (a pay rise, job security, longer breaks) but some baristas in the US demanded the right to bear arms at work.

Some partners have started writing to me for advice, which I am only too happy to provide.

....................................................................................................................

Dear Triple Rosetta,

I am a barista in a very busy store and would very much like to be a Shift Supervisor. For four months now I have been overlooked for a promotion even though I am reliable, hardworking and the customers like me. I suspect my manager has a personal vendetta against me. She doesn't appreciate all the hard work I've been putting in and demands more and more of me each week. What should I do? I tried under-extracting but I don't think anyone noticed. I really want to quit but I am afraid I won't find another job.

Barista Babe.

....................................................................................................................

Dear Barista Babe,

If no one noticed you were unde- extracting, you are
wasting your time making coffee for peasants and should
quit immediately. Your manager must be punished for not
recognising your true worth. Before you leave, steal something
that will do financial damage to the store but for which you
cannot be blamed, like the steam wand nozzle. Because it is
small and easy to misplace, you can claim you left it soaking
in a cup of espresso cleaner and that it must have been thrown
away by accident. How many spare steam wands have you seen
in your store? How long will it take your manager to secure
another one? How many sales will be lost during that time? If
we all contributed in this small way, the company would suffer,
as we suffer.

Yours Sincerely,

Triple Rosetta.

Photos of stolen steam wand nozzles have appeared sporadi-
cally throughout the week. Some baristas have gotten creative and
placed them in the middle of famous landmarks; hanging from the
Brooklyn bridge, floating in the Trevi fountain; a *Where's Wally* for the
disenchanted and underpaid.

It was only a matter of time before head office came looking for me.

"Triple Rosetta?" I looked up from the machine to find two men
in bad suits blocking the doorway.

"Are you Triple Rosetta?"

"Who wants to know?"

It turns out a barista in Portugal burnt his hand on the steam wand
attempting to remove the nozzle just after he had made a non-fat latte.
He filed for workers compensation but folded under questioning.
Because he was actually stealing, not only was he refused compensation, he was fired. In an effort to save his job, he showed my recent
posts to his superiors and claimed he thought he was just following orders. Upper Upper Upper Management wanted to have a little
conversation about my role in this.

I have been suspended without pay until they work out what to do with me.


While I've been living on baked beans, my employers have decided to close most of their stores. We each received a letter blaming the Global Financial Crisis and the current economic climate, but most of the partners blame me. We all know what GFC really stands for: Good Fucking Coffee, which is in abundance in Melbourne. They just didn't do their research, which is odd, considering all the research they made me do before getting behind the machine.

The cafe will close by the end of the week and those on a full-time contract will receive a small payout. The rest of us are out on the street.

If I had known that my online activism meant I would be unemployed, and, due to my newfound celebrity status, unemployable, I probably wouldn't have organised the last campaign, which involved streaming 'confessionals' of partners from all over the world, their features and voices distorted as they admitted to using multi-purpose jugs and not giving two shits about the difference between single origin and single pour.

# FASCIST HIPSTER HALL

The lease has been taken over by Regina, of Regina K Public Relations, who intends to re-invent herself as South Yarra's answer to Nigella Lawson. The original owner's wife, with whom Regina shares a Bikram yoga instructor and a colonic irrigation specialist, passed on mine and the new girl's details. Apparently it was during one of these colonic irrigation sessions that Regina had the epiphany that led her to give up PR and take on the food service industry. I agreed to meet her at the café, which was being renovated in a style which can only be described as *industrial vintage teacup chic.*

Regina's hospitality experience is limited to arranging cheese platters and buying expensive vinaigrette. After our first conversation, I realised she thinks owning a cafe will involve drinking coffee, gossiping with customers and selling over-priced bread rolls from the Abbotsford convent. She wants to 'start a dialogue' about ethically sourced vegetables by hosting a series of dinner parties on the terrazzo. Like anyone who watches too many cooking shows, she believes a sprinkling of sumac from the Prahran market transforms poached eggs on toast into traditional Moroccan fare. I believe that it is only a matter of time before the home-made kumquat and lime marmalade is replaced with Cottee's apricot conserve, but for now she's all figs and fetta and artisan ice cream.

While painters whitewashed the walls and carpenters installed shelves made from recycled hardwood, Regina outlined her plans to turn half of the café into a provedore. "I've applied to the local council to have bike racks installed out the front. I think that would make it look more *provincial.*" She has images of people riding home with baskets full of quince paste and truffle oil. I wanted to say, "You will grow to hate the cafe as the tins of sumac collect dust on your produce shelves and your customers use the bike racks to lock up their three thousand-dollar prams." But instead I suggested providing mismatched straw baskets for people purchasing multiple items. She admitted to knowing "absolutely fuck-all about the whole coffee thing" and offered me a full-time position as Executive Barista. She even agreed to buy back my Gaggia from the café on Swanston St when I told her it was vintage.

I decided to stay until I was up to date on the rent.

Regina likes to divide her time between the kitchen and front of house. She treats each day like an informal dinner party; greet custom-ers at door covered in organic flour, run back to kitchen and whip up "a little something" without asking them what they'd like to eat, sit down with them for a quick chat about the food, take their money under duress. This morning she Jamie Olivered the fuck out of a chicken and served it on an old oar salvaged from the Melbourne Grammar rowing club. She placed it on the communal table, made from a work bench salvaged from the Brunswick tram depot, and encouraged customers to "dig in." She doesn't believe in crockery, so they were forced to eat off oversized bread boards. They ignored her as she explained the provenance of the chicken and the lemon it was stuffed with.

The menus are hidden between the covers of old medical text books. There are three pages devoted to Regina's outlook on sustain-ability before you get to breakfast; although it's not really a menu, it's a just a list of ingredients which she may or may not use on any given day.

On the last page she has written "Our coffee is extracted onsite by our Executive Barista on an original Gaggia espresso machine."

I asked her where else the coffee would be extracted if not onsite. She replied, "Somewhere else."


I arrived to work this morning to find two fixies out the front and knew it was going to be a long day. Two suspicious looking men with beards and matching gingham shirts were standing behind my coffee machine. One took a sip from a short black and had an orgasm.

"These Kenyans are taking coffee to a whole new level! We have to syphon this!"

Regina was arranging native flowers in mismatched jam jars at the communal table. "Paul, I want you to meet Simon and Simon, our coffee suppliers."

Simon and Simon run a boutique coffee roasting company out of a converted warehouse in Footscray. To maintain a low carbon footprint, they deliver four kilos at a time on their pushbikes. Their signature blend costs $75 a kilo.

Simon handed me a very short short black. "This will blow your mind."

"Where's the rest of it?"

"People expect different things from an espresso these days, Paul. The culture's changed. A ristretto used to be the variation. Now it's the standard."

While they got off on each other's enthusiasm I had a little tasting of my own: red wine. Hints of squashed grape.

Regina doesn't believe in supporting large soft drink conglomerates, so anyone in need of a cold drink may choose between home-made lemonade and fresh juice. She insists on buying organic, rather than just lying about it, so a cold drink costs thirteen dollars.

She is nonplussed about my Policies and Procedures manual, which she deemed "too corporate" but she has asked me to help her write a treatment for a reality TV show about her midlife career change ("Think *River Café* meets *River Cottage*!"). This explains why she didn't advertise for regular kitchen staff on Seek; she organised auditions through NIDA, WAPA and the VCA. Once again, I must share a confined space with out-of-work actors, but because these ones have only recently graduated, they are incompetent and attention-seeking, but not bitter.

I wrote a treatment with a list of episode outlines, including *While closing the café, the Executive Barista must deal with the fact that none of the chairs match, making stacking them impossible*, and *Teething issues surrounding tap water*. At first, customers were confused by the new water station; we don't have water jugs, we have watering cans. They are old and make the tap water taste like tin, and it is almost impossible not to pour water all over the floor when refilling a glass, but they look amazing lined up on the vintage plant stand on the terrazzo. Which is important, when you have used your PR contacts to secure a feature article in *Gourmet Traveller*. Regina also used her connections to get a four-page spread in the *Melbourne Magazine*'s annual food issue. Last week we posed for a group photo in the kitchen, gathered around the ingredients for a tuna nicoise salad. The left side of my head is obscured by some hanging garlic. For the cover, the tables on the terrazzo were removed and replaced with a portable herb garden; apparently when someone orders an omelette, the chef/VCA grad runs out to the balcony with a pair of vintage scissors for some thyme.

The café has been busy, but isn't making any money, because Regina can't get her head around the concept of profit and loss. Her shopping trips are largely unplanned and very much spur-of-the-moment; when I got to work this morning there was a message on the answering machine telling me that she had gone to the Wesley Hill farmers' market for heirloom tomatoes, and then she was going to a junk shop in Beaufort to look for antique door handles for the ladies' toilet. Last week she spent an entire day at Footscray market trying to track down some red cabbage she had read about in *Delicious* magazine.

It has taken Regina almost a month to accept that there is no money to be made from organic lemonade served in a vintage thermos. She couldn't bear to make the call herself; I contacted Coca Cola and set up an account.

As she made her way back to the kitchen she asked nobody in particular, "What the fuck am I going to do with all these lemons?"

# When life gives you lemons

you open the Lola and Reg pop-up organic lemonade stand. You make your Executive Barista stand on the corner of Swanston and Flinders at 7am with a vintage juicer (Ebay, $149.95) and a stained glass jug (Richmond Salvos, $15.00) and try to interest passers-by in a "little cup of organic goodness." The passers-by are in a rush to get to work, so he is mostly ignored and he says "Fuck this," and throws the lemons, the juicer and the jug in the bin. I told her I was mugged.

After a customer asked to have the dukkah removed from his goats cheese this morning, I found Regina in the office, crying. "Hospitality is a cunt of an industry, Paul. Why didn't anyone tell me that?" Lots of jobs are stressful, but lots of jobs pay enough that you can get a massage or take a holiday to help alleviate the stress. Hospitality, if you stay too long, takes its toll on your mind, your body and your soul as you start to see yourself as one who exists solely to serve others.

I can take advantage of this woman. I don't feel good about it. But then, I don't feel bad about it either.


My treatment was rejected by all the major networks and every producer in Melbourne, but Channel 31 has agreed to help Regina shoot a pilot, tentatively titled *Kitchen on the Yarra*, because she told them the drama school grads in the kitchen were disadvantaged youths from broken homes. She has been on a liver detox diet for three days because "the camera adds ten kilos." This has made her a little irritable. This morning the whole café could hear her as she yelled, "You fucking actors can't take direction! How hard is it to whisk eggs?!"

Usually, Regina avoids confrontation; she prefers to run her business using good old-fashioned passive aggression. She assumes that we are all as excited as her about the café, and sulks if anyone dares to ask about practical things, such as rosters or pay. We can eat whatever we like and she loves to shower the kitchen staff with gifts, oblivious to the fact that organic kale and retro tea strainers do not help pay the rent. In her mind, we are one big happy family, and we will all benefit when she succeeds. Everyone is terrified of her, except the new girl, who is oblivious to anything that isn't a text message or a Facebook post. She gallops between the communal table and the communal couch without a care in the world. I can tell when someone has worked up the courage to ask for money; Regina throws things around the kitchen. Even I chickened out at the last minute. It was unusually quiet and Regina and I were standing behind the pastry cabinet.

"What did you want to talk to me about, Paul?"

Instead of explaining I was worth a lot more than she was paying me, I said, "I was thinking we should get more muffins."

"What, more than four?"

"Maybe six, even eight."

"But we only ever sell four."

"Maybe if we had eight we would sell eight. If we had sixteen…"

"Sixteen!"

"The sky's the limit."

"If we get more muffins, where would we put the friands? I'd have to source another cake stand."

I decided it was easier to pay myself out of the register at the end of each day. This is not the first café I've watched disappear up its own arsehole. It won't be the last.

# First day of shooting

When I pointed out that everyone was miked up except me, the director explained that he wanted to focus on the drama that unfolded in the kitchen. By 'drama' he meant the heavily scripted tension between the sous chef/NIDA grad and the pastry chef/WAPA grad. For the first time in months I missed the dish pig. I actually missed coming to work not knowing if I was going to live or die.

Regina is portrayed as some sort of mother earth figure who helps the younger staff achieve their dreams of producing quality free-range fare. My job is to make coffee for cast and crew.

# Shooting schedule

| Day | Time | Location | Key talent | Description | Props | Notes |
|---|---|---|---|---|---|---|
| Tues | 6.45am | EXT. Footscray market | Regina | Regina attempts to locate Asian eggplant (organic) for Hakka style Asian eggplant dish with mint. | Basket | Stall holders cannot confirm if eggplant is organic or Asian. Confused by waiver; refused to sign. |
| Tues | 9am | INT. Cafe | Regina | Regina prepares Hakka style Asian eggplant dish with mint. | Knife, cutting board, large serving dish | Preparation of dish suspended - no mint. |
| | 11am | EXT. Footscray market | Regina | Regina returns to buy mint. | Basket | Mint not available. Director suggests making dish without mint. |
| | 1230pm | INT. South Yarra IGA | Regina | Regina continues search for mint. | Biodegradable plastic bag | Mint purchased. |
| | 2.30pm | INT. Cafe | Regina | Regina continues Hakka style Asian eggplant dish. | Knife, cutting board, large serving dish | |

The director told me that if they continue to shoot at this pace, they should have a pilot episode in about two years.

After casually mentioning to the producer that I am a writer, I have been given the task of writing a short outline for potential episodes based on what takes place each day.

# Episode 1 - The dinner party

Regina invites 40 of her closest, well connected friends to sample local produce on the terrazzo with matching wines. It's actually a pleasant evening until Regina catches a writer for *the Age* disposing of his tempura sardine into one of her new organic cotton napkins.

"DON'T SPIT IT OUT! THAT'S SIX DOLLARS' WORTH OF SUSTAINABLE FISH!" The mood is ruined as Regina lunges over the communal table to retrieve the sardine, spilling at least one hundred dollars' worth of sustainable wine.

The director, who has it all on camera, assures Regina that it can be fixed in editing.

## Episode 2 - Tutored cupping session

Regina invites Simon and Simon of Simon and Simon's Coffee Roasting to host a coffee tasting event to showcase their new 'micro-lot offering', which they claim will "challenge and astound even the most progressive palates." Other coffee roasters and baristas gather around the communal table and agree that they can taste caramel and raspberry, butterscotch and other things that don't exist in Kenya. One attendee, obviously *not* a coffee roaster or barista states, "It all tastes like coffee. It all needs sugar," and spits his 30mls of single origin into a nearby pot plant.

The director assures Regina that this can be fixed in editing.

## Episode 3 - Regina becomes highly emotional when customers fail to get excited about small batch almond butter

and locks herself in the dry goods cupboard. The staff, aware that the show must go on, continue to work as though nothing has happened. Regina finally emerges after closing time and hands the Executive Barista a note explaining that she has taken a vow of silence, and from now on will only communicate with the staff and crew in writing.

## Episode 4 - Notes

The Executive Barista comes to work to find handwritten notes pinned to every available surface in the café. There is one addressed to him on top of the Gaggia. It is seven pages long. Some words are capitalised for effect, such as DISAPPOINTMENT and BETRAYAL.

Our new uniforms arrived today. People like Regina don't understand
that when you are in the business of serving food, you should only
ever wear black to work. Black aprons. Black pants. Not checked
shirts. Definitely not 100% organic cotton aprons in this season's
khaki designed by Lisa Gorman. Black. Because this is a dirty job.
It is not a glamorous job. It is not a chance to express yourself. It is
a job in which you spill things and drop things and sometimes you
throw things or have things thrown at you and when you are working
four doubles in a row you don't always have the time or the energy to
wash your uniform. Sometimes you don't even have time to take it off;
you get home after a long day and you collapse on the first available
surface, and before you know it your alarm goes off and you have to
drag yourself off the bed/couch/floor and go back to work. I didn't
bother trying to explain this to her. When someone spilt something
on their apron she would hand them a note asking them to change, so
today's filming took a little longer than anticipated.

I usually throw my mail in the bin without opening it, but this
evening I read my statement from Host Plus. I've been paid cash for
most of my working life, so my current superannuation balance is
$34. 07. I decided it was time to take stock of my life. I sent Regina
a text and asked her to meet me after filming for a Very Important
Discussion.

# Very Important Discussion

As Regina came into the office, I laid out all of my Very Important
Documents; invoices from Coca Cola, egg cartons with "Barn laid"
and "Cage eggs" printed on them, and Woolworths receipts for instant
lasagne, margarine and Dutch crepes, definitely not organic.

She looked at me in horror and scrawled on the back of a menu,
*What do you want Paul?*

"Equal air time." I handed her my treatment for an entire episode
devoted to the Executive Barista.

*But this is a show about me and the transformative power of well prepared
food.*

I produced a receipt for 700 grams of sliced gypsy ham and some
Black and Gold cheddar from the IGA.

This morning someone from Channel 31 attached a lapel mic to my apron and set up a small digital camera on top of the coffee machine.

The director asked me not to address the camera every time I made a coffee. "You're not Ferris Bueller."

"And you're not Martin Scorsese, yet here we are."

I spent the rest of the afternoon wondering how a starring role in a low-budget pilot was going to help boost my superannuation. And the director, no doubt, spent the afternoon finding ways to make me look fat on camera.

My mother came into the café during filming. I pretended not to recognise her but she made a point of introducing herself and the director decided it would be good to interview her. She had the nerve to say, "I raised him to have manners but Paul has always been very rude, especially to members of his immediate family. I blame his father." Then she listed all the times I had been rude to her, as though she had committed them to memory knowing that one day she would have the chance to recall them on community television.

After her brief stint as Social Media Manager for the last establishment, the new girl is determined to get paid to be on Facebook all day, and is studying transmedia two days a week. She asked if she could use me for her first assignment.

"I'd like to turn your diary into a blog."

"It's not a diary."

"I'd like to turn your notebook into a blog. Your writing makes me LOL."

She shows me what comes up on Google when she types in 'barista'. It turns out that there are more baristas with blogs than there are writers, and they are all underpaid underachievers just like me. The more prolific ones have managed to turn their daily rants into job opportunities. One even has his own talk show, in which he makes his guests coffee before abusing them.

"An online presence will help you get published. Trust me."

Within an hour I have my first blog post. And within another hour I post my second, because it's strangely addictive, being able to publish without having to deal with publishers. The new girl is right; there are thousands of people who have nothing better to do than read and comment on my narrative of suffering.

"It would be good to include your mother's Urbanspoon reviews."

"It would be good to pretend my mother doesn't exist."

"No, really, she has a huge following. She's been invited to review cafes all over town. We can leverage that."

As I read through my unpublished manuscript and seven Moleskines full of notes, I realised two things: a) I have beautiful handwriting and b) I have matured as a writer. I hardly recognised the person who filled the first notebook. I decided that between blog posts and tweets I would give my novel another go. There was definitely a story there, just not the one I thought I was writing. The new girl was encouraging.

"Next time you submit your book, you'll have this blog to prove that people are interested in what you have to say."

The cast and crew packed up around me, and Regina handed me a note saying she had an appointment with her colonic irrigation specialist and that I would have to close for her.

The new girl waved and said she would text me the details of my new Twitter account.

I watched her pirouette across the park and wondered when she stopped being the new girl and started to take control of her life. While I was busy fighting to stay behind the machine she had found her calling and was pursuing a career outside of hospitality. I was a little jealous of her, but also proud, and it made me think that maybe the world is a Good Place, and that I should try a bit harder to be a Good Person. I considered this as a woman pulled up out the front in a brand-new Lexus and raced up the steps of the terrazzo, obviously desperate for a coffee. Before she could reach the top of the steps I shut the door and turned the sign around to read

## (NOT) SORRY, WE'RE CLOSED.

She banged on the glass and I threatened to call the police.

I turned the lights off so no one could see me as I stacked the chairs and mopped the floor.

As I backwashed the Gaggia, soaked the group handles and wiped the steam wand, I realised that my longest relationship has been with this machine. It has served me well, but it was time to move on. I stepped away from the Gaggia, half washed, removed my holster and dropped my apron on the floor, imagining the dramatic score that would accompany this scene when my blog/novel was adapted for Broadway.

I didn't bother to quit, I just left.

..................................................................................................

To Whom It May Concern,

Please find attached a copy of my manuscript Hospitality! I am
thirty three and this is my first book. I'd like to think that the
past ten years, which I have spent working in a series of second
rate dining establishments, have not been a complete waste,
as they have provided me with lots of material for this story.
Writing this book has made me realise a few hard truths about
myself, and given me the confidence to do other things.

I hope you like it.

Yours Sincerely,

Paul Whelan.

..................................................................................................

# Paul Whelan

*Curriculum Vitae (abridged version)*

**e.** triplerosetta@gmail.com.au

*"It takes something more than intelligence to act intelligently."* -Fyodor Dostoevsky, *Crime and Punishment*

---

I am a Barista/Writer with over five years' experience in a busy Italian-feel, European-style cafe/restaurant/bar. I have a strong worth ethic, sound knowledge of and commitment to occupational health and safety and do not suffer fools. I am seeking long-term employment with a reputable establishment within 2kms of the Melbourne CBD.

---

## Education

Bachelor of Arts, Swinburne University (to be completed)

CERT IV Coffee Making, Holmsglen TAFE

Barista Basics, Melbourne Coffee Academy

Master Barista, Melbourne Coffee Academy

Wine Appreciation – Basic, Centre for Adult Education, Melbourne

Wine Appreciation – Intermediate, Centre for Adult Education, Melbourne

Novel Writing – Centre of Adult Education

## Employment History

**2006 – present** Cafe Cinque cafe/restaurant/bar

Executive Barista

**Duties**

☐   producing quality espresso based coffees for discerning clientele

☐   writing, editing and upholding Policies and Procedures Manual

☐   planning and implementation of staff training programs

☐   stock control

☐   quality control

☐   crowd control

☐   addressing customer complaints

☐   writing cafe newsletters, menus and specials board

☐   hiring, firing

**Skills**

☐   optimising milk usage

☐   free dosing

☐   free pouring

☐   latte art

☐   multitasking

☐   delegation

**Hobbies** – none

**Interests** – Russian literature, 18th century English poetry, 17th century art, social media for political purposes/action

**Publications**

☐   Cafe Cinque Policies and Procedures manual (2007, 2008, 2009, 2010, 2011, 2012)

☐   An inquiry into the recent trend towards semi-skimmed milk, *Bean Scene* magazine, issue 47, April 2009

☐   The devastating long-term effects of standing behind a coffee machine for twelve hours a day, *Bean Scene* magazine, issue 56, December 2011

*Complete CV, references, writing samples, photos of latte art available upon request.*

# Thank you!

Mel, Jenn, Tom and Kieran who read all the drafts and helped turn
my rant into a story.
Chris, for understanding that sometimes I put the book first, and
for marrying me anyway.
And of course, the real Paul Whelan, my favourite barista-slash-
actor-slash writer, who never let me on the coffee machine, and who
left hospitality in the most dramatic way possible.

www.ingramcontent.com/pod-product-compliance
Lightning Source LLC
Chambersburg PA
CBHW060752050426
42449CB00008B/1376